Things You Won't Believe About Music

Scott Cowie

ISBN: 9781986147897

DEDICATION

For my hot wife Sheryl

CONTENTS

INTRODUCTION

I couldn't find a book that included strange music facts and anecdotes, so I decided to write one. My friend, Martin Kelly used to draw funny pictures to make me laugh at university, so I asked him to draw the pictures for my book. In all honesty, this book is leagues above Shakespeare, Dickens, and any of these so-called "authors" that the world will soon be embarrassed to have held in high regard. Martin's illustrations make Van Gogh look like a monkey with a paint palette. Thank you for showing an interest in this book and please spread the good word. Enjoy xx

1

Pythagoras and Music

Do you ever stop and wonder what you will be remembered for? Do you ever stop and wonder what has been your most significant contribution to the world? In years to come when someone mentions your name, what will those listening immediately think? More importantly, how would you like to be remembered?

Our views and opinions on famous people in history have been accumulated by a number of factors from what we were taught in school, what we have read in books, what we have read on the internet and the general information provided to us or that we have sought out ourselves.

On the subject of music, there are many artists and bands that are remembered for one hit album or even one hit single. In some cases, this can be a nuisance to the act. They may have evolved musically, yet the public still remember them for a certain song or album in which the act may feel doesn't necessarily define them musically.

When you hear the name 'Pythagoras', what springs to mind? What is he best known for? Many know him as simply the 'triangle guy', or you may be familiar with Pythagoras Theorem. It wouldn't be a stretch however to suggest that Pythagoras's extremely significant contribution to the history of music has been significantly overlooked, overlooked to the extent that he is the first installment in the things you won't believe about music.

With the musical instruments and technology we have available to us today, and assuming you don't have perfect pitch, anyone can randomly sing one note and then find what that specific note is by using a piano, keyboard, guitar or even an app on your phone.

As you will no doubt be aware, we have a system in which letters and numbers are assigned to each pitch, a system that has been developed over thousands of years.

Greek philosopher, teacher and mathematician Pythagoras of Samos was born around 570 BC. To give some perspective, this is nearly 2000 years prior to the invention of the harpsichord, and around 2300 years before the piano's invention. Although flutes and harps had existed around European countries such as Greece and Egypt for a considerable time, relatively speaking musical instrumentation was very much in its infancy, certainly from a mathematical and systematic standpoint. No musical note had been assigned a known value or letter. Cue Pythagoras. To this day we don't have an idea of what Pythagoras looked like. Although this picture does portray him as an ugly bastard, the modern fashionable beard signifies that he was very ahead of his time, therefore this balances out.

Legend has it that he was walking past the blacksmith's one afternoon and the sound of the workers hammering anvils caught his attention. Given that many anvils of different sizes were being struck at the same time, with different sized hammers, this lead to different pitches occurring simultaneously. The curious philosopher was also intrigued by how on certain occasions, two different pitches could sound harmonious and all-round "together", yet another two pitches combined could have the opposite and more unpleasant effect. This is what we now recognise as consonant and dissonant.

Pythagoras instantly became fascinated by the distance between two pitches and began his quest of measuring and calculating these distances through a number of experiments. He built a monochord, which is largely accepted to have been invented by him. A monochord is a musical instrument made up of a metal string, which is stretched over a hollow resonating body. Pythagoras attached different weighted strings to the monochord, the heavier the string, the deeper the sound. He discovered that a note's pitch is inversely proportional to the length of the string. Pythagoras continually tried to achieve the same pitch he had heard the day he walked past the blacksmith's.

He also used other methods to work out different pitches, such as pouring different amounts of water in separate glasses. The more water you pour into a glass, the deeper the sound the glass makes. This is an experiment you can easily try yourself with wine glasses.

Pour water in the glass and dip your finger into the water, then slowly glide your finger round the rim of the glass and it will resonate a certain pitch. Then try making sound with two glasses at once to achieve harmony.

The distance between two pitches in music is what's now known as an interval. The specific interval that Pythagoras deemed to be perfect is listed here.

To be clear on two fronts, nowadays this interval is demonstrated in modern music notation as shown in this next example.

In this timeframe there was no music notation. Secondly, there is no way of telling what key Pythagoras calculated this interval in, as this was before the existence of keys/clefs/key signatures as we now know them. For demonstration purposes, we will use the key of C, given there are no sharps and flats in this key (more on this later).

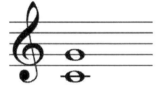

This interval is known as a perfect fifth, it has a frequency ratio of 3:2. It includes the first to the last of a successive five notes in a diatonic scale. The two notes listed are C and G. The five successive notes in this instance are C, D, E, F and G. The description, known to this day as a perfect interval, is a tip of the hat to Pythagoras given he described the sound of the notes played together as being in perfect harmony. It is also commonly known as the Pythagorean interval.

Delving deeper into his obsession with distances in notes, he made another groundbreaking discovery that would have a lasting effect on music, one that every guitarist on earth can be grateful for.

As stated earlier, given a note's pitch is inversely proportional to the length of the string, if you halve the length of the string, you achieve the same note, only one octave higher. An octave is an interval, where both notes have the same note name but with 12 semitones between them.

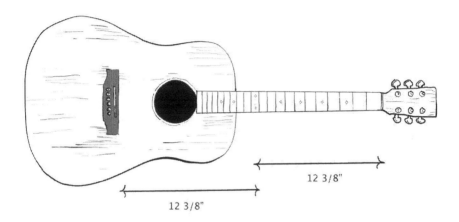

12 3/8"

12 3/8"

Guitarists can create this by positioning their finger on the 12th fret, which is precisely half the length of the string. This is one octave higher than when you would play the string with no finger on the fret at all.

What this means is, if you play one half of the string, you achieve two times the vibration of the string and the wave has less distance to travel, so it vibrates twice as fast. The result is that the note being played is one octave higher.

To this day, every electric and acoustic guitar all over the world is built ensuring that there is equal distance from the nut of the guitar to the 12th fret, and equal distance between the 12th fret and the bridge.

Similarly, if you take a piece of metal that is 20 inches long and strike that piece of metal, it makes a note. For talking's sake, let's assume that note is a C. If you take another piece of metal exactly half the length of the original, in this case 10 inches long, it makes a sound one octave higher, which would be a higher C. Considering that this was another one of Pythagoras's discoveries, then it is safe to assume that he is also responsible for the origins of the glockenspiel and xylophone, given that it is built upon these mathematical equations.

To take this one stage further, given that an octave has a ratio of 2/1, as mentioned earlier, a perfect 5th has a ratio of 2/3. So for example, if you have a glockenspiel, and take low C note, the perfect 5th to the C would be G. The G note is exactly two thirds of the size of the lower C.

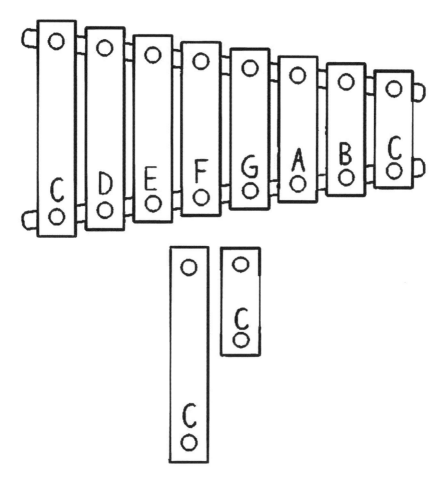

You will also notice in the picture that the smaller C note is exactly half the length of the bigger (lower) C note. Once again, this is known as an octave.

Interestingly the word 'octave', stems from the word octo, which means 'eight' in Latin. Around 60% of the words in the English language are from French/Latin origin. This is largely down to William Duke of Normandy and his army of Normans invading of England in 1066. After taking over and subsequently ruling England, the Normans started embedding their own French/Latin vocabulary into English.

Latin words such as octagon and octopus correlate with the word eight. An octagon has eight sides and an octopus has eight legs. When you start thinking of other words in English starting with 'Oct' and attempt to figure out their relation to eight, you'll perhaps stumble on the word October.

October is the tenth month of the year, however, when the calendar was originally written by Romulus, the first king of Rome, there were only ten months in a year with the inclusion of 304 days. Romulus decided that winter was to be a season with no months. The original calendar, written in Latin, reads Martius, Aprilis, Maius, Junius, Quintilis, Sextilis, September, October, November and December. You'll notice the obvious similarities between the Roman calendar and the modern day calendar, which is known as the Gregorian calendar. In the Roman calendar, October is the eighth month.

The relationship between the word 'octave' and eight in music terms is as follows:

It is essentially the interval of eight diatonic degrees between two tones of the same name. The higher of the two notes contains twice as many vibrations. As a result, an octave is also known as a perfect eighth.

In summary, Pythagoras's contribution to the foundations of music can never be overlooked, as his findings are seen to this day to such a degree that every guitar, glockenspiel, and xylophone are built based on his calculations. It is fair to say, Pythagoras was pretty gangster for his time.

2

Benjamin Franklin's Glass Harmonica

Similar to Pythagoras, perhaps another person whose versatility and diversity in so many different areas caused some of their achievements to be overlooked, was Benjamin Franklin. Franklin was one of the five men who drafted the Declaration of Independence for the United States of America. He was also chosen specifically to represent America in negotiating the 1783 treaty of Paris, which contributed immensely to the end of the Revolutionary War. Given that these credentials led Franklin to be known as one of the Founding Fathers of the United States, one could be forgiven for not believing the extent of Franklin's contribution to music.

Astonishingly, Franklin only attended two years of grammar school, yet he had an insatiable thirst for knowledge, which resulted in him working as a scientist, writer, inventor, printer and politician among other careers. Like Pythagoras, he too was one smart bastard.

Whilst residing in England in 1757, Franklin attended an event in which he saw a musician performing melodies on wine glasses, using the technique outlined earlier. The harmonious vibration of the glasses left a lasting impression on Franklin. He began experimenting at home with his own wine glass set, but became frustrated that he couldn't quite gauge the appropriate amounts of water to pour into each glass to achieve the relevant notes and pitches.

He was of the mindset, that if each of the glasses were the appropriate size in the first place, then there would be no need for long periods of water tuning. Franklin began putting together what was to become the armonica. Also known as a glass harmonica, it contained thirty-seven glass bowls carefully mounted on an iron spindle, largest to smallest. The spindle was operated by a foot pedal and each bowl was colour coded relative to the pitch. The notes were A (dark blue), B (purple), C (red), D (orange), E (yellow), F (green), G (blue), and accidentals were all marked in white. The bowls would rotate whilst the operator rubbed the rims of the glasses to produce a sound very similar to the wine glasses.

America's founding father attended dinner parties and performed on the armonica for various friends. The social circles Franklin kept ensured word spread quickly about the invention to the point that hundreds of thousands of armonicas were made and subsequently sold.

Female musician Marianne Davies who performed frequently throughout Europe, ended up giving armonica lessons to the Queen of France, Marie Antoinette.

This is where it gets really crazy. Both Mozart and Beethoven were both influenced by the sound of Franklin's invention to the extent where both classical musicians composed respective pieces on the instrument. Beethoven wrote a short melodrama, whereas Mozart composed two pieces, namely 'Adagio and Rondo 617.'

Unsurprisingly, Franklin was a workaholic and he included his daily schedule within his autobiography, which ended up being published in 1791, one year after his death.

The schedule showed that Franklin woke up at 5am every morning, and prompted himself with one question, 'What good shall I do this day?' This was set to give him direction for the duration of the day and if other distractions came up, he would have his initial goals to remain focused on. The schedule then followed with a plan to complete more substantial tasks, which he would break down into sub tasks. He assigned himself two work blocks and in between these would have his lunch hour in which he would still perform what he referred to as 'shallow work', which included looking over his accounts and so on. The day ended with the evening question, 'What good have I done today?' Setting aside time for this daily self-reflection ensured Franklin had a deep understanding of the areas that he felt he was successful in, and where he felt he could improve, naturally making those adjustments for the following day.

Given that Franklin invented the lightning rod, the Franklin stove, the flexible urinary catheter and bifocal glasses, his love for music shines through given that he always considered his personal favourite invention to be the armonica.

3

Happy Birthday Sang on Mars

As stated by the Guinness Book of World Records, the most recognised song in the English language is 'Happy Birthday To You', or simply 'Happy Birthday'. The story behind the song is an intriguing and fascinating one, which is far from over.

It was written by two American sisters, Patty and Mildred J. Hill in 1893. The sisters resided in Louisville, Kentucky, where Patty worked as a kindergarten principal and Mildred was a piano tutor. Together, they composed a song that could be sung to the children in the classroom at morning time. Originally, the song was called 'Good Morning To All', the melody and chords were identical to the song we are now so familiar with. Patty wrote the lyrics, Mildred wrote the chords and melody. The sisters then published the original version in a book called 'Song Stories for the Kindergarten'.

The lyrics 'Good Morning To All' would eventually be replaced with 'Good Morning To You', it became a hugely popular children's song in the forthcoming years, no one knows when the lyrical change to 'Happy Birthday To You' took place. Historical accounts indicate that it wasn't either of the Hill Sisters that wrote the lyrics to the most updated version.

The melody and lyrics to the updated version 'Happy Birthday' would first appear in print in 1912 but with no copyright symbol to indicate the identity of the composers, this would lead to a lot of confusion as the sisters were none the wiser to how much popularity the song was gaining after the lyric change.

The copyright was first registered in 1935 by the Summy Company, however, the Hill sisters were not credited as the writers. Summy outlined that Preston Ware Orem and Mrs R. R. Forman now owned the copyright.

(Vincent, 2016)

Luckily, the third Hill sister Jessica, had watched the musical 'As Thousands Cheer' by Irving Berlin which included a version of 'Happy Birthday.' Jessica recognised the melody as it was identical to her sisters' composition 'Good Morning To You.'

By that point, Mildred had passed away, but Patty filed a lawsuit for the infringement which was initially dismissed. Jessica persevered and won her sister Patty a share of the rights which were then split between the Summy Company and Patty. Boom!

Warner/Chappell Music purchased the Summy Company in 1988 for 25 million dollars, the chief motivation behind this was so Warner could own the copyright to 'Happy Birthday', undoubtedly a lucrative investment given they would earn around 2 million dollars a year in royalty collections from the song. Considering that royalty payments for music have to be distributed to the copyright holder every time there is a public performance of the song, one can only begin to imagine the amount of times Happy Birthday is sung on a daily basis around the world in public places.

Films, TV shows and adverts have paid thousands of pounds to Warner Music over a lengthy period for the use of a few seconds of the song, making it a very worthwhile investment all those years ago. It has been translated into at least 18 different languages including German, French, Dutch, Korean, Chinese and more. Now that is impressive!

Interestingly, NASA's 'Curiosity Rover' which roams around Mars, was programmed to hum the melody of 'Happy Birthday' every single year on August 6th, given that is when Curiosity first landed on the planet.

When Patty and Mildred Hill sat next to each other on a piano and first composed the song in 1893 to please a handful of kindergarteners, it is highly doubtful that they would have believed that it not only would it become the most profitable piece of music in the world's history, but it would be the first piece of music to be performed on a different planet. Would you have believed that?

4

Bob Marley's Song Pays for Soup Kitchen

It is perhaps ironic that Bob Marley, a man who advocated for peace, love and harmony worldwide, was born the same year World War II ended. The reggae icon was even granted a Peace Medal of the Third World in 1978 by the United Nations. Marley's musical credentials speak for themselves, but his kindness and generosity is something that connected with millions of fans globally.

Perhaps Marley's most famous song is 'No Woman, No Cry', which was initially released in 1974 and has become not just a reggae anthem, but one of the most recognised songs in popular music, being covered by everyone from Pearl Jam and Nina Simone, to Linkin Park and Billy Ocean.

One thing you might not believe, is that Bob Marley did not want to receive one penny of royalties from the song. In fact, despite writing the track, he isn't even credited for doing so. The person credited for writing 'No Woman, No Cry' is Vincent Ford. Ford owned a soup kitchen in Kingston, Jamaica and was a lifelong friend of Marley.

Bob Marley and his band the Wailers were signed by Island Records. Marley became increasingly concerned over a songwriting contract he had signed previously with producer Danny Sims at Cayman Music, which was still causing legal issues.

After a fall out regarding royalties, Marley decided that he did not want his new songs to be associated with Cayman.

In an attempt to establish a loophole around publishing legalities and restrictions, whilst also providing a better living for those around him, it was alleged that Marley started crediting his songs to close friends and family members such as his wife, Rita, members of the band and so on.

(Sherwin, 2014)

In 1974, Marley wrote "No Woman, No Cry" in Ford's flat at a late night jam session in which Ford was present, though he did not participate in the writing of the song. The most famous version of the song appeared on a live album in 1975.

This was one of three Marley tracks that Ford was given credit for writing, 'Rastaman Vibration' and 'Roots, Rock, Reggae' which was Marley's first hit in the United States.

Through the songwriting royalties, Ford was able to keep his soup kitchen in Kingston, and he lived just behind the Bob Marley Museum up until his death in 2008.

5

Albert Einstein the Violinist

Perhaps the most famous scientist to have ever lived was German born Albert Einstein. In 1905, the then 26 year old transformed the way we view physics and cosmology by publishing a document on special relativity.

Einstein's views were contradictory to the theories of Isaac Newton, which up until this point were widely accepted as fact. Newton was of the opinion that space and time were universally fixed and could not be deviated and Einstein realised that this could not possibly apply if you travelled at the speed of light. To convey this message effectively, Einstein used a now famous 'thought experiment' known as the twin paradox.

If you were to have a set of twins, put one of the twins on a rocket ship and travel to space keeping the other twin on earth, the twin on the rocket ship will naturally be accelerating closer to the speed of light, therefore their time would slow down, meaning that when they returned to earth, they wouldn't have aged as much as the twin who remained on earth the entire time. In summary, the twin travelling will inadvertently be slowing his/her own time down.

Einstein's theory of relativity was revolutionary, what is not as commonly known, is that the world renowned scientist was also a violinist.

Young Einstein was six years old when his mother, who was a classical pianist, encouraged him to take violin lessons. A slow starter, it took some time before Einstein fell in love with the instrument, but when he did, he became obsessed. His two favourite composers were Mozart and Bach. Many experts suggest that Einstein's theories are in keeping with his most loved composer's work, given the clarity, simplicity, creative yet methodical approach has many parallels to the way Einstein believed messages should be conveyed.

In the 1930's, Einstein was one of the most recognised celebrities on earth. Right in the midst of Nazi Germany, he decided to immigrate to the USA, settling down with his second wife Elsa. Despite accepting and subsequently committing to many guest appearances all over the world, he ensured that each Wednesday night was kept free in his diary, given that him and his wife Elsa, would host jam sessions at their home. Some of the world's best known musicians such as violinist Fritz Kreisler and cellist Gregor Piatigorsky would frequently make appearances at the sessions.

There is debate to this day as to Einstein's level of competency on the instrument, but it is widely accepted that he could 'hold his own' as it were, improvising adequately in jazz and blues music and performing many classical pieces. Although his ability is debated, his level of intelligence is certainly not, he might well have been the smartest musician to have ever lived.

On the subject of violins, the bridge of the violin isn't actually glued to the violin. It is held there by the tension of the strings, so that everything vibrates and creates a beautiful, round, resonant sound. I learned this from my friend Nora Germain who is one of the greatest violinists on earth. Check her music out, after you have read this book of course.

6

Django Reinhardt and the Nazis

Guitarist Django Reinhardt remains a hugely influential figure in the jazz world even decades after his death.

Born Jean Reinhardt on the 23rd of January, 1910 in Liberchies, Belgium, Reinhardt started playing banjo and guitar at a very early age, however his career was under serious threat after a freak accident in 1928. He and his wife were staying in a caravan which caught fire after Django knocked over a candle. The couple managed to escape but Django's left hand was very badly burned to the extent that he only had feeling in two fingers.

Despite this, Reinhardt adapted his technique accordingly and became one of the first ever musicians in jazz music to use the guitar as a lead instrument. Prior to this it was predominantly used as a rhythm instrument. He became a pioneer in the style of gypsy jazz, which is a combination of American swing, jazz, Eastern European folk and French dance hall musette.

The musical partnership he struck up with violinist Stéphane Grappelli became legendary. Their collective compositional and improvisational skills made for an extremely in demand live act all over Europe in the 1930's.

After World War II broke out in 1939, Reinhardt's life was again under threat. The Germans had invaded France where he was residing, and given that he and his family were Gypsies, this was an incredibly stressful time. The Nazis were rounding up thousands of Gypsies just like Django in concentration camps and murdering them in large numbers. Django made various attempts to escape from France but was stopped at the borders on each occasion.

Remarkably, after he was captured, he was recognised by the Nazi officers and they subsequently gave him free rein to perform for them across many clubs in and around Paris.

Django's career flourished during this time and he made the most profit of his career during a time where an estimated 600,000 of his fellow Gypsies were being persecuted. Hitler was a very angry man, but even he loved a bit of Django.

7

The Star-Spangled Banner is an Old English Tavern Song

A national anthem is a patriotic song or hymn which generally speaking, evokes the traditions and overall history of the country that it represents.

Many of these national anthems have very interesting stories behind them and can range from one extreme to another as far as length and overall content.

The longest national anthem is the Greek national anthem, titled "Hymn to Liberty", which has a total of 158 verses. Written in 1823, it wasn't until 1865 that there became a shortened version, which included just the first 3 of the 158 verses. Interestingly, this national anthem is also used by Cyprus, which to this day does not have an anthem of its own.

On the contrary, the Japanese national anthem is the shortest national anthem with only 4 lines included in its entirety. This, however, still contains 4 more lines than the Spanish national anthem which has no lyrics at all. It is the only instrumental national anthem in the world. The South African anthem contains a total of 5 languages: Xhosa, Zulu, Sesotho, Afrikaans and English.

The national anthems of India and Bangladesh were actually written by the same writer, Rabindranath Tagore.

The Finland and Estonia national anthems are identical in melody but different in lyrics.

Fascinatingly, 19 days before his death, Mozart wrote an instrumental piece called Freimaurerkantate, K. 623. It is to this melody that the Austrian national anthem is sung.

The very first national anthem was the British national anthem. It is unclear who wrote the lyrics or melody but it has been occasionally attributed to John Bull, although this is still widely debated.

It too has an interesting past as it stems from the phrase "God save the King" which was used as part of a coronation anthem for King Edgar in 973. The first full lyrics appeared in the Gentleman's Magazine in 1745 and was first sung in the September of that year after Bonnie Prince Charlie's invasion and subsequent victory over King George's army in a battle near Edinburgh.

The early version of the song has a sixth verse which is anti-Scottish, with the line "And like a torrent rush, Rebellious Scots to crush."

It officially became the national anthem in the 1780's. Many different verses have been written over the years to suit certain political agenda and by this point it was changed to "God Save the Queen" because of the different monarch ruling.

As it was the first national anthem, and given the extent of the British empire ruling at the time, other countries started using the same melody, or even both the same melody and lyrics for their own national anthems. This melody was used in Denmark, Russia and many German state.. As the decades progressed, different nations started replacing it with their own freshly written anthems although to this day the Liechtenstein national anthem has the identical melody of "God Save the Queen".

It is also one of two national anthems used by New Zealand as of 1977.

Lastly, the song itself has been performed the most times in one single performance. This was in 1909 in Germany when the public were waiting for the arrival of King Edward the 7th. The German band started playing the anthem but the King was still getting ready. To avoid an awkward silence before he was presented, they played the anthem 17 times.

Bizarrely, America was another country who used the "God Save the Queen" melody for their hugely patriotic song titled "My Country 'Tis of Thee".

America's national anthem, "The Star-Spangled Banner" has been used only since 1931 as the official anthem. This replaced the then national anthem "Hail, Columbia."

The lyrics for "The Star-Spangled Banner" were written in 1814 by Francis Scott Key, who was a lawyer and amateur poet. It was initially written as a poem and not in song format.

The music wasn't added until much later by Key's brother-in-law Joseph H. Nicholson. Nicholson recognised that the lyrics would fit the melody from a song called 'The Anacreontic Song' which was written by a British composer named John Stafford Smith.

'The Anacreontic Song' was written back in 1773 and acted as the official song for the Anacreontic society, a popular Gentlemen's club in London which Smith was a part of. Essentially, the origin of the American national anthem was that of an old English tavern song. The song was popular on both sides of the Atlantic and Nicholson identified the melody as a perfect fit for his brother-in-law's poem. It took one hundred years after it was written, but on the 4th of March 1931 after several failed attempts to have the bill passed, "The Star-Spangled Banner" became the official American national anthem.

8

The Planets Sing in Harmony

This chapter is likely to make you feel very stupid. This is simply because Kepler was so smart. He was smarter than everyone around him. On a daily basis Kepler probably felt similar to how you and I feel being around drunk people when we are sober. Just for the record, you're not stupid so please don't get upset with that opening line.

In 1619, German mathematician and astronomer Johannes Kepler published a book called 'Harmonices Mundi', which is Latin for The Harmony of the World. Kepler's outlook was that given every object that vibrates is essentially emitting sound, from the electrons moving around the nucleus of an atom to massive tubular bells, that surely planets would fall into that category too.

Given that planets are huge moving/vibrating objects, Kepler was convinced that they must be emitting some form of sound.

Skeptics immediately dismissed the theories stating that sound requires air in order to travel, and considering that there is no air in space, there would be no sound to detect in the first place. Kepler, however, proclaimed that the planets would still be emitting electromagnetic vibrations and despite the fact that there is no air in space for sound to travel, it wouldn't necessarily mean that planets weren't still emitting sound, only that scientists hadn't yet developed the technology that could detect it.

Legend has it that Pythagoras originated the initial idea, claiming he could actually hear the music of the spheres and that the ancient Egyptian God Thoth had given him this ability.

Taking it a stage further, Kepler went as far as calculating the sound of each planet, taking into account their size and their minimal and maximal orbital velocities around the sun.

He discovered that the orbits are not perfectly circular, and that the sun is slightly off centre in planetary orbits. The planets move faster when they are closer to the sun and slower when they are furthest away. Kepler stated that not only would the planets emit sound while they turned around the sun, but the sounds were also propositional to their speeds, and their continual pitches would rise and fall smoothly like sirens or like musical scales.

Mercury is the smallest and fastest planet in the solar system and is also the closest planet to the sun. This, combined with the planet's drastic temperature changes which range from 427 degrees Celsius during the day, to minus 173 degrees Celsius at night, ensures the considerable change in pitch that the planet emits. Despite the change in pitch, it still remains an octave higher than the next two planets in line.

The two sister planets, Venus and Earth, have nearly circular orbits, the range of Venus is only around a quarter tone, and the range of Earth is around a half tone. Kepler stated that the Earth sings Mi, Fa, Mi.

Sound of the Planets (and Moon)

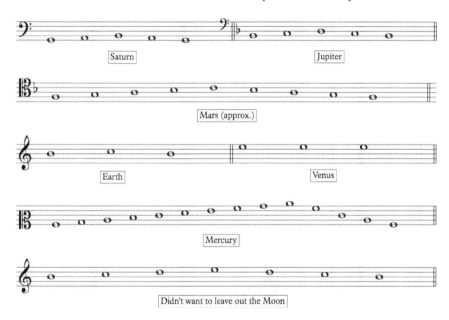

These two planets constantly change between major and minor chords, with Mars playing the tonic (lower) note of the triad.

(Kepler, 1619)

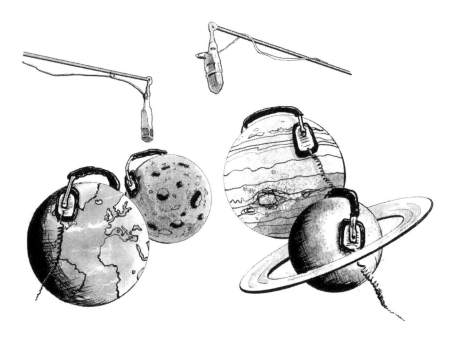

At the time of writing his publication, mankind only knew of six planets: Mercury, Venus, Earth, Saturn, Jupiter and Mars.

The celestial choir Kepler observed contained Mars, which acted as the tenor, Saturn and Jupiter as the two basses, Mercury in the role of the soprano, and Venus and Earth acting as the two altos.

Kepler came to the conclusion that in cosmic time, the planets in their orbits at the closest to the sun, or the furthest away from the sun, will be the largest number of consecutive consonant events. In simple terms, the planets are most in tune with each other when they are closest to the sun, and furthest away from the sun.

Amazingly, Kepler's eyesight was actually very poor, to the extent that he struggled to see through a telescope, which makes it all the more impressive that he was able to calculate these findings with such limited technology. To this day, NASA with their massive advancements in technology, have determined Kepler's calculations to be scarily accurate.

9

Eminem's Verdict Is Rapped By a Judge In Court

It sounds too ridiculous to be true, but every word of it is. It actually sounds farfetched to the extent that it would be laughed at if you suggested it as a scene for a movie, but as the old saying goes, the truth is stranger than fiction.

Detroit born rapper Marshall Mathers, more famously known as Eminem, released his second album titled The Slim Shady LP in February 1999. On a song titled 'Brain Damage', Mathers rapped about his experiences with a school bully named D'Angelo Bailey. Throughout the rap Eminem claimed he was bullied regularly and unmercifully by Bailey, being thrown in lockers and having his nose broken against a urinal.

Below is an extract from the song.

"I was harassed daily by this fat kid named D'Angelo Bailey

An eighth grader who acted obnoxious, 'cause his father boxes

So every day he'd shove me in the lockers

One day he came in the bathroom when I was pissin'

And had me in the position to beat me into submission

He banged my head against the urinal 'til he broke my nose."

In 2001, Bailey tried to sue Eminem, claiming that the song painted him in a false light and that the disparaging comments had damaged his reputation.

Eminem's lawyer responded by determining Bailey an 'opportunist' trying to cash in on Mather's success.

Interestingly, evidence of Bailey's bullying was backed up by Eminem's mother, who filed a lawsuit against the Roseville school district in 1982 over several incidents between Eminem and Bailey. She claimed that the beatings her son received had various lasting mental effects such as insomnia, nightmares and antisocial behaviour. These papers were accessible in Eminem's defence. The alleged bully denied all claims in Eminem's rap.

Luckily for Mathers, Judge Deborah Servitto dismissed the accusations by Bailey, claiming there would be no grounds for a lawsuit.

The real intriguing aspect of this story was that, in a very bizarre fashion, the verdict was delivered in a 33 line rap.

Here is Judge Deborah Servitto's entire verdict (rap) below:

"Mr Bailey complains that his rap is trash

So he's seeking compensation in the form of cash.

Bailey thinks he's entitled to some monetary gain

Because Eminem used his name in vain.

Eminem says Bailey used to throw him around

Beat him up in the john, shoved his face in the ground.

Eminem contends that his rap is protected

By the rights guaranteed by the first amendment.

Eminem maintains that the story is true

And that Bailey beat him black and blue.

In the alternative he states that the story is phoney

And a reasonable person would think it's baloney

The court must always balance the rights

Of a defendant and one placed in a false light

If the plaintiff presents no questions of fact

To dismiss is the only acceptable act

If the language used is anything but pleasin'

It must be highly objectionable to a person of reason.

Even if objectionable and causing offense

Self-help is the first line of defence.

Yet when Bailey actually spoke to the press what do you think he didn't address?

Those false-light charges that is so disturbed

Prompted from Bailey not a single word.

So highly objectionable. It could not be – Bailey was happy to hear his name on a CD.

Bailey also admitted he was a bully in youth

Which makes what Marshall said substantial truth.

This doctrine is a defence well known and renders Bailey's case substantially blown.

The lyrics are stories no one would take as fact

They're an exaggeration of a childish act.

Any reasonable person could clearly see

That the lyrics could only be hyperbole

It is therefore this court's ultimate position

That Eminem is entitled to summary disposition."

Bailey's attorney wasn't very complimentary, stating "I'm shocked that a judge would do that."

Servitto expressed that she wanted to have the verdict in a language that was universally accepted.

To this day, Eminem and the judge have not yet planned to record a collaboration album.

10

A Death Metal Band with a Parrot as Lead Vocalist

Waldo the Parrot is his name, and fronting a death metal band is his game. The band in question is Hatebeak, formed by drummer Blake Harrison and guitarist/bassist Mark Sloan.

The three piece whose goal is to "raise the bar for extreme music" are signed to Reptilian Records. The band actually split up for a period of time (the parrot didn't go solo) but they reunited in 2015 to release the album 'Number of the Beakon.'

Blake and Mark played in various different bands prior to the formation of Hatebeak, but wanted to be a little more creative with their music so decided to pursue the vocal capabilities of Waldo.

The 21-year old African Grey Parrot and the band have never toured due to the obvious complications that would ensue, but the Baltimore based three-piece studio project is going from strength to strength, with a total of five studio albums, millions of views on YouTube and a strong social media presence. The band's sound has been described as "a jackhammer being ground in a compactor" which does sound very positive.

Hatebeak have actually recorded an album with a band called Caninus, whose two lead singers naturally are dogs, although Hatebeak can claim to be the only band who are fronted by a bird.

11

The World's Longest Concert Will Last 639 Years

The World's longest concert will last 639 years. It's actually ongoing as you read this, unless you are reading this in the year 2640 or after. ASLSP (As Slow As Possible) is a piece composed by John Cage with the intent of becoming the longest piece of music ever performed. The piece was initially written in 1987 and the original piano version lasts between 20-70 minutes. As the title of the piece suggests, it is performed very slowly and contains long sustained notes and chords with very occasional changes. Due to the unique requirements of the piece, this self-playing organ was built specially in 2009 and it is held in the St. Burchardi Church in Germany. It is a massive, stupid looking wooden object with two pipes attached to either side, with weighted sandbags holding down the notes for years.

Prior to 2001, there were many versions of the piece performed by different artists such as Diane Luchese, who performed a 14 hour and 56-minute version, and Joe Drew who has performed a full 24-hour version.

The performance began in the St. Burchardi Church on September 5th, 2001. There was not a chord change until July 5th 2005, which would be a guitarist's nightmare.

The third change happened on January 5th, 2006 which meant 2006 was an extremely active year for the organ, as there were a total of 3 chord changes.

A chord change is like a massive event, and people travel from around the world to see it. This is not sarcasm, just watch YouTube.

As this book is written, the next chord change occurs in 2020 so it is probably a good thing that the organ plays itself as it would be a long gig for any pianist. There is an official website for the ASLSP, you can go and listen to extracts from the piece of music. This is not recommended though because it's horrendous. It sounds like a cross between the noise of a cheap hoover and a dinosaur taking a dump, but not as melodic.

12

Music was an Olympic Sport

Believe it or not, music was once a category in the Olympics. This spanned over a period of thirty-six years from 1912 to 1948. There was actually a total of five arts categories; painting, sculpture, architecture, literature and music.

Baron De Coubertin, considered by many as the founding father of the International Olympic Committee, had pushed for the arts to be included for years prior to 1912, battling against many organisers for their involvement.

Coubertin was faced with the argument that art is too subjective, which leads to great difficulty on occasions defining and judging what is 'better'. This is partly the reason it is so hard to believe that an art form like music could be judged on this stage, let alone it being considered a sport. If that's not crazy enough, here's where the story gets even better.

The Olympic committee decided that it would be appropriate for all of the musicians who were participating to compose their music with an Olympic theme.

Also, similar to the sports, participants couldn't be professional musicians, they had to be at an amateur level. This in itself is difficult to establish, as there has never been a system that distinguishes a professional musician from an amateur.

If that's not odd enough, the music was not actually judged on performance or even by judges listening to the piece, the compositions were judged by the music score that was submitted.

Naturally, given music comes in a form that is best heard (it's insane this has to even be justified) and given the Olympics is such a visual spectacle, it is odd to imagine they wouldn't look to capitalise on music being performed at the event.

Further categories were developed within music over time, such as mixed music, compositions for orchestra, soloists, chorus, vocalists, instrumental and chamber music.

Furthermore, many of the judges on the panel couldn't read or write music and to top it all off, there were even occasions in which the judges decided that none of the compositions were good enough to win medals, so there were no awards given.

On a side note, Paul McCartney performed two songs to open up the 2012 Olympics. Do you know how much he got paid? Have a guess. McCartney and his band were paid $1.57. Essentially he offered his services for nothing, given, performing to an estimated 1 billion viewers is smart marketing, but there had to be a fee put forward for contractual purposes. It appears music and the Olympics have always had a strange relationship.

13

Bach Wrote Songs to Help Fight the Coffee Ban

The next time you make yourself a cup of coffee, be grateful you don't get your head chopped off. The reason being that coffee has been banned numerous times throughout history. Before we talk about Bach, let's look at some occasions in which coffee ban attempts were made.

In 1511, the governor of Mecca banned coffee as he believed it stimulated radical thinking to the extent that it would unite the opposition against him.

Over 100 years later in 1623, Sultan Murad Han, known as Murad, or
Murad the IV, claimed the Ottoman throne that year. An extremely
aggressive and paranoid man, Murad would continuously walk the
streets of Istanbul in plain clothes, disguising himself to mingle with
the general public to assess their perception of him and his ruling. To
his dismay, he found out that not only were there elements of
discontent, but talk of rebellion against him. These discussions tended
to be in the social setting of coffee houses. Murad wasn't happy that
people were gossiping and speaking negatively about him and the more
coffee houses he visited the more it appeared to be the houses that
called for potential rebellion against his ruling. He decided to intervene
by banning coffee and tobacco, then eventually alcohol.

Whilst wandering the streets, if Murad saw anyone breaking the law by
drinking coffee, he would physically punish them on the spot,
everything from a beating to beheading.

Despite banning alcohol, ironically Murad drank a lot himself and
ended up dying with cirrhosis of the liver.

During the 16th century, clergymen deemed coffee to be satanic and
demanded it to be banned. This was soon overruled by Pope Clement
VIII who tried coffee and loved it. He even went so far as to baptise
it. That's not a joke.

In 1675, King Charles II not only banned coffee houses and coffee
itself, but anyone selling coffee, tea, chocolate or sherbet. Luckily the
ban didn't last long.

Johann Sebastian Bach, an avid coffee lover, decided to write a piece of music called the 'Coffee Cantata', which poked fun at the coffee ban and that its 'notoriety'.

Bach performed the piece with an ensemble in a coffee house called Zimmermann Café in Leipzig, Germany. Bach was actually the musical director of that coffee house for over 10 years. That means you could go into this small yet rowdy coffee house during this time, drink coffee and watch Johann Sebastian Bach, one of the most credible and talented composers that ever lived, host performances free of charge and occasionally perform himself.

Translated into English, the Coffee Cantata goes like this:

"Father sir, but do not be so harsh
If I couldn't, three times a day,
Be allowed to drink my little cup of coffee,
In my anguish I will turn into
a shriveled-up roast goat
Ah! How sweet coffee tastes,
More delicious than a thousand kisses,
Milder than muscatel wine.
Coffee, I have to have coffee,
And, if someone wants to pamper me,
Ah, then bring me coffee as a gift!"

14

Man Receives Disability Benefits for his Heavy Metal Addiction

Sweden born Roger Tullgren is officially classified as disabled due to his addiction to heavy metal. This was following the results of a psychological analysis which led to the 42 year old being granted additional funding to supplement his income.

The obsession started when his older brother brought home a Black Sabbath album in 1971 and Tullgren has been hooked on the genre ever since. He has become so passionate about heavy metal that the obsession impacted negatively on almost every aspect of his life. He attends around 300 shows per year and listens to the music "24 hours a day", skipping work regularly which has led to frequent job losses.

The ageing rocker was convinced that his obsession with the genre was a disease, so began pursuing an official route to be categorised as handicapped. After initially being dismissed, he spoke to three different psychologists and they finally agreed to provide help to, in Tullgren's words, "avoid being discriminated against."

He started working part time as a dishwasher in a restaurant in his home town of Hässleholm and the employment service agreed to pay part of his salary while his boss gave him a special dispensation to play loud music at work. Under the new ruling, he was also allowed to wear his own clothes which usually would not be suitable for the job, including band T-shirts and his various tattoos and skull and crossbones jewellery.

His previous employer became tired of his absences and Tullgren was left jobless and reliant on welfare handouts.

The sessions with the occupational psychologist resulted in a solution for both parties: Tullgren signed a piece of paper on which his heavy metal lifestyle was classified as a disability, an assessment that entitles him to a wage supplement from the job centre.

Part of the form reads:

'Roger feels compelled to show his heavy metal style. This puts him in a difficult situation in the labour market. Therefore he needs extra financial help'.

The manager at his new workplace allows him to go to concerts as long as he makes up for lost time at a later date, and more importantly, he gets to listen to heavy metal while washing the dishes.

He also plays guitar and bass in two rock bands. It would have been the icing on the cake if it was two jazz bands, but it's still a great story. (Cooper, 2015)

15

Franz Liszt: The World's First Rock Star

Franz Liszt is not a name that's ever really associated with rock and roll, but in many regards, this Hungarian/Austrian composer was the world's first rock star.

Born on the 22nd of October 1811, in Raiding,Austria, Liszt received piano lessons at the age of 7, and soon began composing and subsequently performing and touring. Liszt was a child prodigy and he was able to play Mozart's entire repertoire by the time he was 11. He travelled across Europe, performing a mixture of his own compositions and others' work at various different concerts.

After his father died, Liszt moved to Paris to share an apartment with his mother. His musical career was about to take a very significant turn. He attended a charity concert run by Niccolò Paganini, a virtuoso violinist who was also renowned for his fantastic stage presence and performance. Stay tuned for more on Paganini later.

Liszt was blown away, and decided that night he would dedicate himself to becoming the 'Paganini of the Piano'.

The Hungarian started playing his whole repertoire solely on piano, which was very rare at the time, turning the piano sideways to give the audience a better view of him performing. With his long hair and eccentric movements while performing, he was determined to become the greatest showman of his generation.

With this in mind, Liszt was also the first known performer to play an entire concert of his own compositions without sheet music, performing entirely from memory. This was considered quite a feat given the complexity of the pieces.

The compositions themselves were completely different in form to the music of Mozart and Beethoven. Liszt essentially veered from classical forms and created a structure that would eventually be known as thematic transformation. This is a technique that involves developing a melody or theme by transposition/modulation and/or augmentation. It is essentially a technique of variation, a basic theme is reprised throughout a work of music, but the theme undergoes constant transformation, disguised and appearing in contrasting roles throughout the piece.

Despite this being a technique that Beethoven had touched upon in his fifth symphony, Liszt took this to a different extreme. This form is used today in almost every film score.

Liszt was undoubtedly groundbreaking in many different aspects, and Kings and Queens worldwide would request Liszt to play at their palaces, which signifies his popularity.

On this note, one thing that was very striking was the level of fan hysteria present at Liszt's concerts. He played to fanatical female reaction to the extent that so many fans were begging for his hair clippings, he hired a dog whose fur he would shear off and send as his own.

The level of female fan reaction eventually led to the term 'Lisztomania' being coined to describe the hysteria at Liszt's performances, years prior to the term 'Beatlemania' being used to describe the reaction to the Beatles phenomenon and their fans' reaction to the group.

These are just some of the key elements that led to Franz Liszt being coined 'The World's First Rock Star', not to mention the fact that he toured Europe for a total of eight years from 1839 to 1847. This undoubtedly would put The Rolling Stones, Metallica, U2 and others to shame. It would also make one hell of a tour T-shirt.

Liszt legend lives on. The next time you hear Bohemian Rhapsody, think of Franz Liszt, as Queen named the song after a well-known Listz piece called Hungarian Rhapsody. Queen actually released a live album/concert film named Hungarian Rhapsody: Live in Budapest. This is a tip of the hat to eight year tour veteran himself, The World's First Rock Star: Franz Liszt.

16

Abba Wore Stupid Costumes to Avoid Paying Tax

Even though it was in the midst of 1970's flower power, and even though Abba's costumes were designed to ensure the group stood out, the main motivation for Abba's elaborate and outrageous onstage costume design was for tax reasons.

Believe it or not, there were laws within the Swedish tax code which allowed the cost of the outfits to be deducted against tax as long as they were so ridiculous that they could not possibly be worn on the street.

Essentially this means that Abba could claim the outfits as an expense relating to their work provided that they looked completely outrageous.

Ironically, the glittering hot pants, sequined jumpsuits and platform heels became a huge influence on 70's fashion and were so culturally accepted to the extent that many people were wearing similar costumes to emulate their heroes.

The Swedish outfit shot to fame in 1974 after winning the Eurovision song contest with 'Waterloo.' On a side note, they managed to beat fourth place UK entry Olivia Newton-John.

It seems the Swedish authorities would attempt to seek revenge on Abba, as band member Björn Ulvaeus was actually taken to court and subsequently accused of failing to pay an estimated £7.9 million in taxes between 1999 and 2005. He did, however, win his case and although they may have looked stupid onstage, Abba were a crafty bunch with their finances.

17

Slipknot Sue Burger King

The title of this chapter allows the imagination to run wild, to the point where the imagery that springs to mind would make for great artwork that our future grandchildren can look back on and wonder what the hell happened to our absurd generation.

Global fast food franchise Burger King have had a history of creating bizarre and creative marketing campaigns. In 2004 they decided to promote their "Get chicken the way you like it" campaign by having a subservient chicken on their website. The said chicken came in the form of a man dressed in a large chicken suit who would appear through webcam, giving the impression he was following any command you set through your computer. This was cleverly carried out as the commands were pre-set. Astonishingly there were over 300 pre-set commands, including 'sleep', 'backflip', 'act like a dog', to name just a few.

That same year, Burger King, using the same advertising agency "Crispin Porter + Bogusky" (CPB for short) decided to produce a campaign to promote their new chicken fries. They created a mock metal band called "Coq Roq". The band had their own website and Myspace page. The coqroq.com website (don't bother looking, it's no longer there) featured an image saying "Groupies Love The Coq."

There were six members of the Coq Roq group who, despite being loosely dressed as "badass chickens", they looked extremely similar to heavy metal band Slipknot, whose very distinctive image includes each member having their own signature style mask. Just like Slipknot, the Coq Roq band also featured one member wearing a gas mask, a kabuki-style face covering, and a mask with dreadlocks attached.

The band featured the following members:

Vocals: Fowl Mouth
Lead Guitar: The Talisman
Rhythm Guitar: Kabuki
Bass: Free Range
Fire Breather: Firebird
Drums: Sub-Sonic

Coq Roq had a handful of original songs, two of which the group made video commercials for, "Bob Your Head" and "Cross the Road". "Bob Your Head" features the band performing live in what is a very Slipknot-feel gig. Within the video the band also beat up a clown that resembles McDonald's mascot Ronald McDonald after he offers the band chicken nuggets.

Here's where the plot thickens. Shortly after the second commercial was released, Slipknot's lawyers responded on August 4th 2005 by filing a cease and desist letter. Slipknot stated that using a band to pass off the image and persona of them came as no coincidence. They also claimed that CPB (Burger King's agency) had already contacted them in 2004 with the intent of having Slipknot appear in a Burger King advert. They went on to claim that Burger King had expressed interest in tapping into Slipknot's teenage fan base and overall large audience. After weeks of discussion, Slipknot rejected the idea of being associated with Burger King. Within the letter, Slipknot also stated that in spite of rejecting this affiliation, Burger King had chosen to create a lookalike, soundalike "band" in order to influence their audience to purchase chicken fries, and that the Slipknot audience had expressed their anger and confusion over several message boards and social media, saying that the group were "selling out" by being part of this campaign.

Slipknot claimed that the whole ordeal constituted multiple violations of the rights of publicity of the individual members of their band, coupled with obvious trademark infringement. They demanded that Burger King and CPB immediately cease and desist from any further advertising using the image and likeness of Slipknot, including taking down the websites all within 5 days of the letter being received. Failure to comply with those demands would result in a lawsuit in which Slipknot would be entitled to an award of Burger King's profits through the campaign.

Burger King argued back, stating that they were not infringing on Slipknot's trademarks and publicity rights. They claimed that there are many groups who wear masks and even makeup to accomplish a mask-like effect, including but not limited to bands such as Kiss, Insane Clown Posse, Mudvayne and Mushroomhead.

The case was thrown out of court in August of the same year, as the judge ruled that there was no infringement on any right of Slipknot's publicity or trademark. One can't help but think there was a trick missed here. If only the court case could have been a ticketed broadcast live on MTV with guest judge Ozzy Osbourne, surely huge profits would have been made.

If you are a fan of both fast food and metal, and Ozzy for that matter, there is a fast food parody metal cover band named Mac Sabbath, fronted by Ronald Osbourne, who are based in Los Angeles. They are more than worth checking out.

18

Amazing Scientific Effects on the Brain While Playing Music

Music has existed in all cultures throughout history, dating back thousands of years. What is it that the human race find so addictive and gratifying about music?

In essence, music is a combination of audio frequencies and complex patterns which float around the airwaves and into your brain. Similar to how your eyes process light, your ears process sound and can trigger a state of excitement in your brain.

Over the past few decades neuroscientists have made revolutionary breakthroughs in understanding in greater detail what goes on in the brain while someone plays a musical instrument.

These tests have been carried out using instruments such as FMRI and PET scanners. When people are hooked up to these devices, traditionally, activities such as reading and undertaking math problems each have corresponding areas of the brain where activity can be observed.

Interestingly, when tests were carried out on people listening to music, scientists saw what they later described as 'fireworks' going off. Many areas of the brain were lighting up as the people were processing sound. The brain's activity while taking into account different melodies and rhythms was very apparent.

The next logical step was for scientists to carry out tests on a musician's brain while they performed music. They discovered that playing music is the brain's equivalent to a full body workout. Neuroscientists saw multiple areas of the brain lighting up at incredible rates.

Whilst playing music, the brain simultaneously processes different information in extremely intricate and complex sequences.

If you are wondering exactly what it is about making music that sets the brain alight, neuroscientists have outlined that practically every area of the brain is engaged at once, particularly the visual, auditory and motor cortices. Disciplined rehearsals and practice in playing an instrument strengthens those brain functions, and enable us to apply the strengths in other non-related music related activities.

Performing music requires fine motor skills, which are controlled in both hemispheres of the brain. This activity combines the linguistic and mathematical precision in which the left hemisphere is more involved, while the right side of the brain, traditionally the more creative side, is obviously achieving a great workout given the creative nature that music entails.

Overall, music has been found to greatly increase the activity in the brain's corpus callosum, which is the bridge between the two hemispheres. This allows messages to travel across the brain faster and through more diverse routes.

Therefore reading, performing and creating music at great length, could in turn help musicians solve problems in a more creative manner in social and academic settings.

Studies have also shown that musicians' memory systems work on a higher level and that they can create, store and retrieve memories more quickly and efficiently than others. Musicians appear to use their well-connected brains to give memories numerous tags, such as an audio tag, an emotional tag, a conceptual tag and a contextual tag.

Despite numerous studies on people performing different sports or arts, musicians on many occasions have demonstrated the highest level of cognitive function and neural processing.

19

Prince Played 27 Instruments on Debut Album

Aged only 20 years old, Prince released his debut album and performed every single instrument on it. That would be 27 instruments in total.

Prince was one talented bastard. Born Prince Rogers Nelson to very musical parents, he wrote his first song called "Funk Machine" on his father's piano when he was only 7 years old. A mere few years later, he recorded a demo tape and was subsequently signed to Warner Music aged 17.

What would follow would be nothing short of a glittering career, including eight Grammy Awards, a Golden Globe, an Academy Award for the film "Purple Rain", and an induction into the Rock and Roll Hall of Fame.

While Prince was in the midst of selling 100 million records of his own, he managed to find the time to write some songs for other artists including "Nothing Compares 2 U" by Sinéad O'Connor and "I Feel For You" by Chaka Khan.

He also changed his name to a symbol, but it's likely you already knew that. The chances are you don't know all of the 27 different instruments he played on the debut album, so here they are:

1. Electric Guitar

2. Acoustic Guitar

3. Bass

4. Bass Synth

5. Singing Bass

6. Fuzz Bass

7. Electric Piano

8. Acoustic Piano

9. MiniMoog

10. PlyMoog

11. ARP String Ensemble

12. ARP Pro Soloist

13. Oberheim Four-Voice

14. Clavinet

15. Drums

16. Syndrum

17. Water Drums

18. Slapsticks

19. Bongos

20. Congas

21. Finger Cymbals

22. Wind Chimes

23. Orchestra Bells

24. Wood Blocks

25. Brush Taps

26. Bell Tree

27. Glockenspiel

20

The Drummer from Def Leppard
Only Has One Arm

This next entry is one incredibly inspiring story which perhaps puts a lot of everyday life simplicities we take for granted into perspective. Formidable drummer Rick Allen joined the band Def Leppard on November 1st 1978, the day of his 15th birthday. Exactly one year later, he celebrated his 16th birthday with a performance at the famous Hammersmith Odeon in London, supporting AC/DC.

Leppard were produced by Robert John "Mutt" Lange and rose to fame during this period, regularly opening for Ozzy Osbourne and Blackfoot.

After a well-received first album, years of touring, it seemed that nothing could go wrong for the English rock group, or for the young and now extremely wealthy drummer, who was fulfilling a dream he'd had since he was 9 years old.

In 1984, Allen had come home to Sheffield for the Christmas holidays, and on the 31st of December, he and his girlfriend decided to go for a drive a few miles out of Sheffield in the countryside in his Corvette Stingray.

He then got into an unfortunate incident with a fellow driver. The driver was moving far too slow for Allen's liking and yet still wouldn't let him overtake. Allen lost his temper, subsequently lost control of the car, then hit a dry stone wall and entered a field, causing the car to roll over several times. During this, the improperly fastened seat belt was only attached to Allen's left arm. Allen shot out of the car window, however the seat belt jammed his left arm in and caused it to be severed from the rest of his body.

Also, and this is a part of the story that isn't so well publicised, Allen's right shoulder was very badly damaged in the accident too. Allen's girlfriend suffered minor head injuries and bruises.

In the coming days after this tragic incident, doctors reattached Allen's left arm, however the arm soon became infected, which resulted in them removing it once more.

This would be a tragedy for anyone to go through, let alone someone whose career and livelihood was seemingly dependant on having use of both arms. What happened next is truly spectacular.

Still in hospital, and with the help of a friend, Allen started to design an electronic drum kit which would incorporate a left foot pedal that could trigger a snare drum sound. For anyone who doesn't know, the snare drum is the drum which sits between the drummer's legs, which generally speaking in rock music, predominantly gets hit with the left hand. He then designed a total of three different pedals which would trigger sounds compensating for the beats his left hand would have played.

Another complication was that the electronic kit needed to be small and compact given that Allen's right arm was still limited after his shoulder injury. The right shoulder blade was in such bad condition he couldn't lift the right arm up fully.

There were many months after the incident where Allen would become extremely frustrated while playing, his left foot just couldn't do what his brain was commanding. Essentially his left foot was carrying the load his left hand once was, but it was a slow process.

To add to Allen's upset, Def Leppard were receiving a lot of calls from other drummers subtly hinting that they were available for the job. "How's Rick doing?" seemed to be the semi-sincere question.

Allen's sheer determination and spirit knew no boundaries and he spent hours, days, weeks and months getting used to the new setup. He took small steps every day and battled through the hours of frustration and simply never gave up.

Eventually he joined Def Leppard in a rehearsal and the band have since described it as unbelievable watching him play. They took to the stage again and Allen's return was marked in an incredibly emotional moment in 1986, when the band performed at the Monsters of Rock festival in Donington. The thousands in attendance erupted in sheer hysteria when singer Joe Elliott introduced Rick Allen, recognising his willingness and determination to play drums again.

Looking back at the incident, Allen states that in life you have to go through the dark side to really appreciate the good in life, and that hard work and positivity goes a long way. He still tours round the world with Def Leppard to this day, an amazing 34 years after the incident.

"The human spirit is the strongest force I know."

Rick Allen

21

Rock Music Made Dictator Surrender

What song do you find to be so irritating that you just can't listen to it? Or do you have two or three that get on your nerves to the point where you would rather eat tinfoil than listen to another nanosecond of it? Don't worry, that's perfectly normal.

But let's just say you didn't have any tinfoil nearby. What would happen if someone were to play your most hated piece of music non-stop for hours, days or even weeks?

This is not necessarily a go-to torture method, but it has its uses when it comes to dealing with dictators.

What better day of the year to pick for this than Christmas Day itself!

1989 was the year, 25th of December, and the man in question was Panamanian General Manuel Noriega. The repressive military leader had holed himself at Vatican's embassy in Panama after President George Bush Senior had invaded Panama.

At the time, Noriega was facing a US indictment with an accusation of drug trafficking, combined with claims that he had rigged that year's election.

US troops surrounded the embassy but Noriega refused to surrender. The US army decided to put down their guns and rolled in huge speakers which they mounted at the walls.

They proceeded to use a wall of sound to blast the dictator until he eventually surrendered.

Featuring on the playlist that day was Guns N' Roses, The Doors, Jimi Hendrix, Iron Maiden and not necessarily in keeping with the hard rock theme, but Martha Reeves.

On the 3rd of January 1990, the general surrendered.

Due to this successful music torture session, the US Army has since repeated this approach.

In 1993, it was successfully used on a cult leader in Texas, after they blared pop music at his compound, and in 2010 the marines reportedly blared heavy metal into villages in Marjah for hours, along with threats to the Taliban.

It is odd that some of the greatest music ever created has been used as a form of torture. Having said that, if a dictator determines being made to listen to Jimi Hendrix as torture, he deserves all he gets.

22

Listening to Mozart Improves Your IQ

They call this the Mozart effect. A set of research results in the early 1990's indicated that listening to Mozart's music leads to short term improvements on selected mental tasks.

The term was first coined by Alfred A. Tomatis and subsequently popularised by author Don Campbell in his book 'The Mozart effect'. The book was based on experiments which showed that listening to Mozart's work would temporarily boost scores on IQ tests which were carried out in America.

As a result, the Governor of Georgia Zell Miller proposed a budget to provide every child in Georgia with a CD of Mozart's music. As a side note to that, in 2016, Mozart's CD sales outsold Beyoncé.

Wolfgang Amadeus Mozart was a very unique person. His list of attributes, achievements and general 'things you wouldn't believe' make for fascinating reading. Here are some below:

- By the age of 5, Mozart was playing the harpsichord and violin professionally. He could write music before he could write words. At 6 years old he performed in front of royalty. He wrote his first symphony at 8 years old, and his first opera when he was 14.

- He wrote half the number of symphonies he would write between the ages of 8 and 19.

- He could listen to music just once and write it down without one mistake.

- Mozart was taught by his father Leopold Mozart. In order to get Mozart out of bed, he would play incomplete scales, ending at the second last note on the scale. Mozart would get out of bed, rush to play the last note to ensure the phrase was complete, therefore he was now up for the day.

- Mozart composed over 600 pieces of music and out of all of his symphonies, only 2 were in minor keys.

One thing about Mozart that is perhaps not so well documented is his sense of humour. Around 1782 he wrote a beautiful composition, so melodic and easy on the ear, yet the title of the piece is "Lick Me In The Arse". These lyrics feature throughout the song. It is rumoured that the lyrics were inspired by a German drama Mozart had seen in which a character uses the phrase as an insult. Mozart was actually a big fan of "Scatological Humour". If you are not familiar with this term, it is simply a posh phrase for "toilet humour".

He also wrote a piece of music called "Ein Musikalischer Spaß" which means "A Musical Joke".

What's so funny about this piece? Well there are subtle little winks, like the purposely badly written violin part at the end of the third movement, but the more obvious joke is at the very end of the piece where Mozart abruptly ends the otherwise beautiful piece of music with a bar of notes in different keys.

23

Man Sells 1900 Tickets for Fake Spice Girls Show to Pay for Nose Job and Sex Change

Out of all the chapter titles in this book, there is a strong case for this one being the most ludicrous and hard to believe, but it is in fact true. The Spice Girls, who have sold over 85 million records worldwide, were undoubtedly a phenomenon that captured the imagination of millions across the globe.

Looking to capitalise on the success was a concert promoter in Hawaii named Akram Abdullah-Wasi (oh and you'll like this, he was previously known as John Lewis). He decided to run a fake concert in the height of Spice Girls fame which was the summer of 1997.

He charged $40 for adults and $25 for students. The fake "Summer Blast 97" festival was advertised to have the Spice Girls headline, and also on the bill were rap group Freak Nasty and Hawaiian locals Sunland.

Suspicions began to arise on the lead up to the festival as there only seemed to be one person responsible for everything regarding the summer spectacular. This would obviously be highly unlikely given it was due to host one of the biggest pop groups in the world at the time. Police contacted the Spice Girls representatives and fraudster Abdullah-Wasi was subsequently arrested. As the police reports show to this day, he claimed he was simply raising funds for a sex change and a nose job.

24

Creed Performed So Badly Their Fans Sued Them

Creed are a band that have always divided opinion, which happens to be a common theme for shit bands.

In 2003, four Creed fans decided to sue the band. This was based on a performance at Chicago's Allstate Arena the previous year. Creed's frontman, Scott Stapp, could not perform given he was so intoxicated and/or medicated.

The fans in question were two couples; Philip and Linda Berenz,and Chad and Wendy Costino. They asked for reimbursement for their four tickets, coupled with parking charges totalling $227. The suit was filed in Cook County Circuit Court on April 22nd 2003.

According to the disgruntled fans, during the performance Stapp left the stage on several occasions during songs for long periods of time. He would roll around the floor in apparent pain or distress. This shouldn't have come as a shock, as this is how most of us react when we hear Creed.

Within the suit, the fans stated the concert was of such a low standard, that they considered it as bad as a no-show. Interestingly, they also requested the court to consider a class-action which would enable the remaining 15,000 in attendance to also receive refunds.

It does make for an interesting debate, whether or not fans have the right to complain if they feel they did not get their money's worth from an act's performance. The natural danger is that given art is so subjective, that's where the issues become all the more complicated: who really decides what's passable, and what is the criteria?

In this instance, the band decided to address the incident through their official website. In good political fashion, they issued a great spin on things. After describing the front man's performance as a rare off night, they continued, "for now, we hope that you can take some solace in the fact that you definitely experienced the most unique of all Creed shows and may have become part of the unusual world of rock and roll history."

Rock and roll history is Freddie Mercury writing Bohemian Rhapsody on his own, not an egotistical singer who doesn't respect his audience enough to able to sit up straight.

The case is still unresolved, but personally I hope they get their money back. Having said

that, they are Creed fans so perhaps they deserved all the poor service they received.

25

Music Makes Plants Grow Faster

Believe it or not, it is specifically classical music which has been determined by research to be a stimulant for plant growth. Experiments have been conducted for many years in the following manner; several of the same plant types are planted, at the same time but in different areas.

One area plays continuous classical music, while the other area plays either different types of music or is left in silence

After a dedicated amount of time, the majority of studies show that it is the plants that are exposed to music that actually grow faster. To take this a stage further, experts realised that there is a certain genre of music that plants are overwhelmingly more responsive to. Can you guess what the genre is? No? Have a guess.

Okay, it's classical music. It should be no surprise that even plants like Mozart and Beethoven.

Author of the research paper "The Sound Of Music", Dorothy Retallack carried out further studies in 1973, with results detailing that plants grow even better when being exposed to North Indian classical music, to the extent where the plants faced the speakers after a period of two days. Conversely, the plants that were exposed to the rock music leaned further away from the speakers, and died after a shorter time. The soothing sound vibrations, particularly within classical music, offer long sustained notes and harmonies which lead to healthier sound waves, something plants respond well to.

Therefore if you are a plant owner, you might want to reassemble your plant playlist based on your new knowledge.

26

Leo Fender, Inventor of the Fender Guitar, Couldn't Play Guitar

Clarence Leo Fender was inducted into the Rock and Roll Hall of Fame in 1992 and strangely enough, throughout his life he never learned to play a single note on the instrument he spent an entire career building.

Aged 13, the young Fender had shown a keen interest in electrics, spending a lot of time in his uncle's shop. He had an almost unnatural knack for fixing the radios that his uncle had built from scratch, particularly when none of the adults in the family, including his uncle, were knowledgeable enough to fix.

His skillset and natural entrepreneurship led him to open up his own radio repair shop in his parents' house, which would eventually be known as 'Fender Radio Service'.

Soon the shop expanded to fixing guitars and amps, but Leo became continuously frustrated with the designs of some of the guitars that he would regularly repair.

This led to further developments in the 1940's as Leo started the 'Fender Electric Manufacturing Company', which is largely referred to simply as 'Fender', and throughout the decade he designed many guitars, basses and amps which are still widely used to this very day. In 1949, he invented the Fender Esquire, then later released an improved version called the Fender Broadcaster. In 1950 another improved version was released which would also become the first mass-produced solid body electric guitar, known as the Fender Telecaster.

Then in 1954 the Fender Stratocaster was released. This went on to become perhaps the most recognised and iconic guitar in the world. Another interesting fact relating to this period is that Fender was contacted by the music company Gretsch, who complained that there was now confusion in the marketplace given that one of their drum kits was also called the Broadcaster. Fearing legal action, Leo decided to stop putting the 'Broadcaster' name on the guitars, and to simply leave the head where the name was written blank, until he thought of a new name.

These 'no-name' Fenders soon became known as 'Nocasters' and are now high level collectors' items. If you want one, you will have to pay somewhere in the region of £50,000. Selling this book after you read it will help a little with that, but not much.

27

The World's Oldest Melody

The Hurrian Hymn, which was discovered in the 1950's on a clay tablet in Ugarit, Syria, is over 3400 years old.

The clay text was found amongst around 30 other tablets of a similar nature, and indicates that the piece of music is to be played on 9 lyre strings and specifies the intervals between those strings.

When musicians nowadays attempt to recreate the ancient piece, it is predominantly played on a modern evocation of the ancient Kinnor Lyre from neighbouring Israel; an instrument almost tonally identical to the wooden asymmetrical lyres played throughout the Middle East at this amazingly distant time when the Pharaoh's still ruled ancient Egypt.

Modern day music notation reads extremely differently to the way the Hurrian Hymn is laid out, given that modern music notation began to develop around 1000 AD.

The melody is a set of instructions for intervals and tuning based around a heptatonic/diatonic scale. Below is a modern day take on the piece, this version is very loosely based on an interpretation by Dr. Richard Dumbrill.

Hurrian Hymn

Arrangement by Scott Cowie

Composer: Unknown

Despite the fact that the lyrics have been difficult to translate, it turns out that the song is dedicated to the Hurrian goddess of the orchards, Nikkal. Modern academics have established this as the closest translation:

'Once I have endeared the deity, she will love me in her heart,

the offer I bring may wholly cover my sin,

bringing sesame oil may work on my behalf in awe may I'

28

Where the Hell Did "Do Re Mi Fa So La Ti Do" Come From?

Have you ever stopped to wonder where "Do Re Mi Fa So La Ti Do" comes from? Well you need not wonder anymore. Have you ever heard of Guido d'Arezzo? No? He was an Italian monk. Trust me, as far as monks go, Guido was pretty damn cool and hugely influential on the history of music, particularly pertaining to music theory, notation and sight-reading.

He was born in a small Italian town called Arezzo, hence the name Guido d'Arezzo which translates to Guido of Arezzo.

At the beginning of the 11th century, Guido wrote a piece of music which became a fundamental building block to the way we teach music to this day. He combined a melody and text, both of which were passed down through generations. The melody itself was said to be derived from the teachings of Pythagoras, and the poem was from a similar time.

To give some perspective, prior to this, music on the whole was taught by rote, which means the teacher would sing the melody over and over again until the pupils would remember it note by note.

Despite this, in ancient Greece, centuries prior to Guido's time, music began to be written down with what were called Neumes. This was a very basic concept in which small squiggly lines appeared above each syllable/lyric of the song/hymn in order to dictate where the melody moved.

Guido, who had the job of training young choristers at the cathedral in Arezzo, felt that there needed to be a better structure for this notation, as there was no indication for rests, rhythms or relative pitches. It would highlight the general shape of the melody but would not be specific to the actual note. Trying to establish a better system, he invented the Guidonian hand, in which different parts of his hand represented alternative notes. He would point to his hand and lead the choir to sing the respective notes.

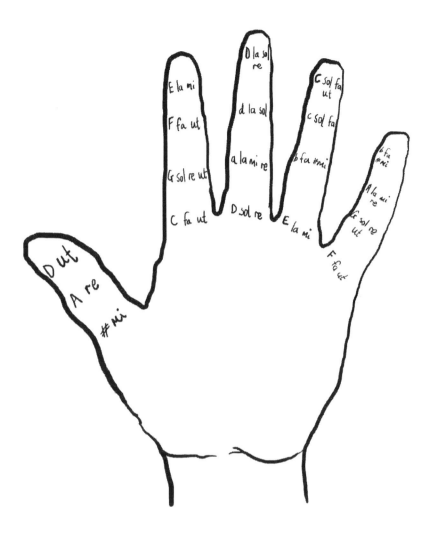

The next step was very crucial, even though there was some evidence of music notation starting to use lines to help with pitching prior to this, it was the smart and intuitive Italian monk himself who essentially created what we now know as the stave. That's the UK term, the American term is the staff. Originally Guido's staff had a total of four lines.

Have a look at the melody that Guido created. The text that he used was from an ancient hymn from the 8th century which was dedicated to John the Baptist.
It translates to "So that your servants may, with loosened voices, resound the wonders of your deeds, clean the guilt from our stained lips, O' Saint John".

Guido d'Arezzo : Ut queant laxis
(11th cent.)

T qué - ant   lá - xis   re - so - ná - re   fi - bris

Mí - ra   ges - to - rum   fá - mu - li   tu - ó - rum,

Sól - ve   pol-lú-ti   lá-bi-i   re - á - tum, Sánc - te   Jo - án - nes.

You will notice that at the start of each phrase I have put the words in bold. The reason for this is that Guido used these specific words and built a scale from it.

The scale reads "Ut Re Mi Fa Sol La".

This became known as the hexachord. It contains notes all separated by a whole tone, expect from Mi and Fa which are only a semitone apart.

There have been only two big changes between the 11th century and today within this system. 'Ut' was replaced with 'Do' as the diction was emphasised better, and 'Ti' was added before the repeated 'Do' note an octave higher.

Here is an updated version of the melody on modern day music notation with a typical 5 line stave and added time signature.

Ut Queant Laxis (Hymn to St. John the Baptist)

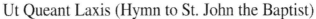

Notation: Scott Cowie   Arr: Guido d'Arezzo

This particular sequence is what is now known in western music as a major scale. It is crucially important to our culture.

Essentially, a scale is a set of musical notes ordered by frequency and/or pitch. To give perhaps a rather bizarre comparison, the rising wail of a siren is an ascending slope of frequency, however a scale can be more likened to a staircase. Dependant on the scale you can take one step, or even two steps at a time. This analogy will make more sense as this chapter progresses.

In contemporary popular music and even western music as a whole, the scales predominantly used have been widely inherited from Greek tradition, known as diatonic scales. The term diatonic means progressing through tones. There are seven tones between each octave, as stated above. That's the same amount of tones the modern day major scale consists of.

Almost all of western music between the late renaissance and the early twentieth century was based on two different forms of the diatonic scale. These two different types of scales are the major and minor scale. Below is the Guido-influenced major scale coupled with the different types of minor scales commonly used within contemporary popular music and beyond.

Major Scale

Natural Minor Scale

Harmonic Minor Scale

Melodic Minor Scale

29

Jesus Christ Fronts a Punk Band and Craps Onstage While Abusing Women

There has been a lot of violence and general controversy associated with punk rock since the birth of the genre in the late 1970's. The same can be said for many forms of music from rock to the hardest of hardcore metal. However, regardless of genre, most live performers that like to walk on the wild side as it were, pale in comparison to a man who was born Jesus Christ Allin, better known by his stage name, GG Allin.

This man makes Marilyn Manson and Eminem look like Cliff Richard. It is important to note that all of these descriptions could be mistaken for glorifying such behaviour. To be clear, that is nowhere near the intention, it's simply another thing you just won't believe about music.

GG got his nickname when his young brother Merle couldn't pronounce his birth name Jesus, and called him Jeje as an alternative, which was soon adopted as GG by all of his friends and eventually became his stage name. Merle would feature later in GG's career as his bass player.

Allin fronted many punk bands in the underground New York punk scene of the 80's and 90's, most notably The Murder Junkies, in which his brother came on board. Most of the time Allin performed live naked and described his audience as the enemy.

"I'm not here to entertain, I am here to annihilate."

This is one of GG's most famous quotes.

His live performances became notorious for the violent, disgusting and disturbing scenes. The naked, bald, tattooed frontman would punch fans, self-mutilate to the extent that he was a bloody mess, and would even perform oral sex with female and male members of the audience as well as urinating. Lastly, and for the lack of a more appropriate and politically correct term, he would regularly take a crap onstage.

Last toilet-talk fact for now; he urinated on the head of his record label at the signing party.

GG threatened to commit suicide live onstage on Halloween 1989 as a sacrifice to rock and roll. There was a spanner in the works for the plan as he ended up in jail on that date.

He was actually arrested more than 52 times in 12 states for a series of crimes, robbing houses being one of them. Allin wasn't the only band member who had brushes with the law. The Murder Junkies' drummer Dino also did time for exposing himself to an underage girl. For what it is worth, Dino also performed live naked too.

Jesus Christ Allin perhaps unsurprisingly had an anti-establishment standpoint on life. He stated that most of the people he saw were like robots, and they were victims of a corporate society who followed unfair rules and regulations that "dumbed them down". GG appeared on live television shows proclaiming himself to be the messiah, and that all children should follow him. He did have a cult-like following in every sense of the word. Fans would flock to see him and worshipped every move he made.

After regular promises to commit suicide onstage, including the 1989 one mentioned earlier, Allin's death was accidental.

His last ever show was in a small club called The Gas Station in Manhattan. The club suffered a power cut after the second song. GG then wrecked the club and ran outside while being chased by a group of fans. He eventually went to a friend's apartment where he and others partied for the remainder of the night. Allin died from a heroin overdose and was pronounced dead on the 28th of June 1993.

Considering all the crude references, violence, nudity and toilet-talk, I decided that it would be best not to have an illustration depicting this chapter. I credit you, the reader, to have a horrible, vile and disgusting enough mind yourself to imagine every last bit of it. Perhaps you could do a drawing of your own as the sound of your creepy, evil laugh fills the room.

30

The Bestselling Musical Instrument in the World is the Harmonica

Yes, it's true. The best selling musical instrument in the world is the harmonica. Given how portable and accessible the instrument is, it shouldn't be too much of a surprise.

Interestingly, it was also the first musical instrument in space.

The Gemini VI spacecraft was launched by NASA in December 1965 on a mission to dock with its sister, the Gemini VII module in outer space. There were two astronauts on board, commander pilot and harmonica player Wally Schirra Jr, and Wally's co-pilot Tom Stafford.

On Christmas Eve, Wally decided to play a joke on his friends down at mission control by telling them that he had seen another spacecraft coming towards them which seemed to be controlled by "a large man with a red suit". Mission control were confused and started panicking. Then Wally started playing "Jingle Bells" on the harmonica with his co-pilot Tom shaking sleigh bells. Both the sleigh bells and harmonica that Wally Schirra played are on display in the Smithsonian National Air and Space Museum, Washington DC.

The harmonica itself is a "Hohner Little Lady", which is the smallest harmonica available, with only four holes, therefore totalling eight notes that can be played.

If you were to go and purchase a harmonica, you can be safe in the knowledge that any harmonica in the world has been handmade.

Every reed in every mouth organ has been finely tuned with a tiny file. The parts are turned out using the same machines that were used 150 years ago.

Invented in the 1900's (although unclear by whom), it is common belief that this happened in Vienna, given that were many harmonica companies, such as Messner and Hohner, dating back to the 1820's.

An estimated 40 million harmonicas have been sold in the USA. If you purchase one yourself, a recommended song to try for the first time is either "Merrily We Roll Along" or the iconic riff in "Love Me Do" by The Beatles.

31

The Devil and Music

The story of Satan and music is extremely deep-routed. Taking into account the history of the art form, the devil does appear with great regularity. He of course features in song titles such as 'Sympathy for the Devil' by the Rolling Stones, 'Devil in Her Heart' by The Beatles, 'Devil's Dance' by Metallica, 'Runnin' with the Devil' by Van Halen, 'The Devil's Beat' by Sandi Thom, not to mention the extent of clever Satan references in legendary guitarist Zal Cleminson's Sin'Dogs critically acclaimed debut album "Volume 1".

Other than being the subject matter in many high profile songs, there is perhaps an even more sinister, eerie element to the relationship with music and Satan that hasn't been as well documented.

Most fans of music will be familiar with the stories of blues legend Robert Johnson selling his soul to the devil, more on that soon, however you would have to go back a few hundred years to track back to when Satan started making an impact on incredibly talented and seemingly vulnerable musicians.

In 1713, the devil appeared in a dream to a well-known classical violinist named Giuseppe Tartini. Within the dream, Tartini made a pact for his soul. He then gave the devil a violin, and the devil performed the most beautiful sonata Tartini had ever heard. Immediately upon waking, he tried to write down from memory what he had heard, and subsequently wrote his most famous work, Violin Sonata in G, better known as the Devil's Trill Sonata. Despite the huge success and general recognition the piece received, Tartini was forever tortured by the experience as he always felt that he never really came close to recreating the Devil's performance in his dream. When describing his own sonata, he stated that it was "so inferior to what I had heard, that if I could have subsisted on other means, I would have broken my violin and abandoned music forever."

The devil's persistence in violinists hadn't weakened even hundreds of years later.

Virtuoso violinist Niccolò Paganini, mentioned earlier, is considered by many to be one of the greatest violinists to have ever lived. He was a trailblazer, an electrifying performer who would command a stage decades before stage presence was a term or even a thought in anyone else's mind. He was a tall, lanky, long yet thin-haired, ridiculously talented soul who was simply years ahead of his time.

He started playing mandolin at age five, began writing his own compositions by the age of seven, and started performing by the time he was twelve.

It later came to fruition that Paganini's mother was so supportive of his music career, that she would stop at nothing to ensure he had the best possible chance to fulfil his lofty musical ambitions, therefore it was actually his mother that was alleged to have made a deal with the devil, trading her son's soul for his chance to be the greatest of all time.

Paganini was so advanced musically and his look made him unlike any performer around in the early nineteenth century. His all-round mystique and eccentricities made the devil- related rumours believable. Audiences far and wide would make the sign of the cross as he performed, to protect themselves from 'evil'. Paganini would break strings while playing then continue to perform regardless, almost fitting the description of 'a man possessed'.

At age fifty four Paganini passed away. Hours before he died he sent away a priest who had come to perform last rites. This act fuelled the rumours of his association with Satan and solidified a nickname that films about his life have been titled after: 'The Devil's Violinist' .

Perhaps one of the most famous myths which has become legendary, is said to have taken place in the Mississippi Delta in the 1920's.

The story goes that a young man named Robert Johnson desperately wanted to become a great blues guitarist, but struggled to even play a blues lick at the time. According to legendary blue's singers/guitarists Son House and Willie Brown, who both knew Johnson, would frequently scold Johnson about his bad guitar playing. They, and any passers by, consistently told Johnson to stop playing as he "made such a racket".

Suddenly, Johnson disappeared, and wasn't seen or heard from in months, and it was assumed that he had run away from his mother and father. There were rumours that he had gone to Arkansas, and some said that it was at this point that he started being taught by guitarist Ike Zimmerman.

After Johnson's long hiatus with no explanation, he suddenly arrived one day in Banks, Mississippi where Son House and his friends would often play and hang out. Everyone was puzzled and inquisitive about Johnson's whereabouts for all those months. They rolled their eyes as Johnson took out his guitar, but their jaws immediately dropped at the staggering ability Johnson demonstrated, compared to when they last heard him.

Johnson had confessed that one night, exactly a minute before midnight at the Mississippi crossroads, he took his guitar and a big black man approached him. It turned out to be the devil. The devil tuned his guitar, played a song and then Johnson made a pact with Satan himself. Exactly where the crossroads are in Mississippi is subject to more speculation. Some say it's in Rosedale, but it is more popularly believed to have been at the junction of US 61 and US 49 in Clarksdale, Mississippi.

Johnson went on to record songs that would become the foundation of blues music and rock and roll. It is worth noting that he references the devil many times in his music.

To this day he remains a hugely influential figure to many, including the likes of John Mayer, B.B. King and Eric Clapton, who regard him as one of the all time greats.

In 1938 Johnson passed away, and was subsequently honoured and inducted into the very first Rock and Roll Hall of Fame in 1986.

The rumours of Robert Johnson's deal with the devil continue to divide opinion, given the story of blues singer Tommy Johnson is almost identical, but many swear that Johnson confessed to selling his soul.

Another element of the relationship between the devil and music that cannot be ignored is the consistent satanic imagery that seems to be ever-present within metal music. Where this stems from is down to individual opinion, but a theory that perhaps cannot be taken off of the table is that of the Devil's Tritone. "What in the name of Lucifer is the Devil's Tritone?!" I hear you scream.

The Devil's Tritone is a musical interval. As we know from chapter 1, an interval is the distance between two notes/pitches, sometimes intervals are consonant and harmonious, sometimes they are dissonant and eerie. As you would expect, the Devil's Tritone is dissonant and eerie. Also known as the augmented 4th or diminished 5th, it's named the tritone because it spans over three whole tone intervals. It perfectly divides an octave into two equal parts.

The controversy surrounding the tritone dates back hundreds and hundreds of years prior to metal music however, and even further back than 1713, when the devil haunted Giuseppe Tartini in his dreams. In fact it dates all the way back to the middle ages (medieval period) of the 5th to the 15th century, before our system of tonal harmony. The majority of music composed back then was written for the Catholic Church. As a result of the tritone sounding so unresolved and dissonant, church officials across Europe assumed there was a ghostly relationship with the devil within the music. Therefore the Latin phrase "Diabolus in Musica", which means the Devil in Music, was born.

The same church officials were so afraid that if monks were to sing the tritone, the devil himself would appear. There is no hard evidence to prove whether or not this was the case, but rumour has it that the Devil's Tritone was banned in numerous catholic churches as a result of this.

From the medieval period right up until this date, sinister yet beautiful music has been created by using the Devil's Tritone, such as Après Une Lecture Du Dante by Franz Liszt, "Enter Sandman" by Metallica, and the opening of "Purple Haze" by Jimi Hendrix.

It's also worth noting that "Diabolus in Musica" is also the title of the 1998 album by heavy metal band Slayer. The album itself is, without question, in the dissonant and eerie category.

It is strange to think that there are numerous relationships between music and the devil spanning well over one thousand years, and perhaps this last one is the most controversial of them all. You can decide if there's any sort of connection here, but The Holy Bible itself does state that Satan was once in charge of music in heaven prior to becoming a fallen angel who betrayed the Lord. What do you think?

32

Music Royalties

How much money musicians get paid has been a controversial subject, particularly in recent years as a result of the internet, and in particular the music streaming phenomenon. The way music is distributed and consumed is significantly different to how it was in the past. Although the distribution of vinyl has been on the up, in many ways it has represented and flown the flag for a forever dying physical form of distribution.

Physical distribution is vast becoming a thing of the past, largely due to a smartphone generation which enables music to be streamed, therefore less and less money is being paid for the consumer to enjoy music, which in turns means less and less money is going to the artists creating the music. The money that goes to the artist is known as royalties. There are two different types of royalties: mechanical royalties and performance royalties.

Performance royalties are distributed every time an artist's song is played in public; in a bar, pub, stadium and so on. This is not restricted to a live performance, so if a song is being played on the jukebox in a local pub, a small percentage is paid to the artist. Even when a song is heard on the radio, a performance royalty is paid to the artist every time the track is played, which is why every venue that plays music must have a PRS licence.

Mechanical royalties are paid by whoever obtains a mechanical license to reproduce and distribute a piece of music, which includes everything from a digital download to a CD. A mechanical royalty is paid to the songwriter. However, the term mechanical royalty has a rather fascinating background. It is a term that has been around for over one hundred years, and it is a story that is rarely told.

In the early 1900's it was commonplace for many pianists to earn almost all of their living going from bar to bar performing various different pieces, including self-composed material. This of course still happens to this day, but it was even more prominent back then. To quantify, this is fifty years prior to Elvis and the rock and roll period, so the industry as we know it now was very much in its infancy.

In the late 18th century there came the invention of the Player Piano, which was in essence a self-playing piano. It looked exactly like a piano, although with one significant difference. Each song the piano played would require a different piano roll which would work the mechanics inside the piano. The rolls would have small bumps, similar to reading braille, or when you record a piano part on the programme GarageBand and you can click on it to see what keys are being played at certain points.

The Player Piano was a fantastic invention if you were a club/bar/restaurant owner, as it meant they did not have to pay a musician to provide entertainment. They would purchase a Player Piano, then buy the relevant rolls for whatever songs they wanted played. Musicians were displeased to say the least. The first reason for their discontent is an obvious one; they were losing out on a lot of work as a result of the invention. Secondly though, they were not receiving any royalties for the songs being used. For example, if you were to buy the piano roll for the song "The Entertainer" by Scott Joplin, and have the song played in your venue, Scott Joplin would not receive a penny for it.

Musicians were up in arms over this and took legal action, stating a breach of copyright. Their argument was that if copying sheet music was illegal, then so would be the illegal copying and subsequent distribution of piano rolls including the same music. At first, the authorities determined that there was no breach of copyright as there was no human that could read the piano rolls. Eventually, in 1909, it was granted that musicians would be paid for every copy made of the music in piano rolls. From that point on, this was known as a "Mechanical Right", named after the mechanics of the piano. This is a term still used over one hundred years later.

33

Acts You Won't Believe Never Had a Number One Hit

Developments in technology have resulted in massive changes in the way that music in consumed this century. High increases in streaming music across many different platforms, from Spotify to YouTube, have led to question marks raised over whether or not chart positions have the same value as in previous years. In the UK, the official chart countdown still takes place every Sunday. Although the show is still popular, it can be argued that there is not as big an incentive for artists to achieve the top spot as in years gone by. It was a huge feather in the cap for so many bands and artists to achieve a number one single. Blur and Oasis had a huge battle in the mid-nineties, releasing respective singles on the same day to claim the top spot, which Blur won.

In 2009, in a bid to overthrow the X Factor's dominance over the Christmas number 1 spot, an online campaign was created by a couple in England to attempt to have Rage Against The Machine's "Killing In The Name" beat The X Factor's winner to the top spot. This anti-X Factor campaign was successful.

There are however, many acts who, despite having massively successful careers spanning over decades, bizarrely haven't achieved a number one hit. Being huge in many different countries and even, in some cases, selling out arenas and stadiums across the globe has strangely not led to a number one hit at least once in their career. Here is the list of all the noteworthy bands/artists that didn't quite make it to the top spot.

The Smiths

The highest chart position The Smiths reached was number eight in a 1992 re-release of "This Charming Man". Perhaps this has led to tension between the band members which has resulted in them never reforming? That is a joke for any lawsuit-happy lawyers.

Bon Jovi

A string of huge hits across the globe for decades after their formation in 1983, but never a number one. "Always", "Livin' On A Prayer" and "Dead Or Alive" were hits of a generation but not once did the 80's icons top the charts.

Alanis Morissette

The mezzo-soprano Canadian singer has had hits since the early 1990's, but the top spot has always eluded her. Another fact about Alanis Morissette, is that Foo Fighters drummer Taylor Hawkins toured with her before upping sticks and joining Dave and the gang.

Led Zeppelin

They headlined Knebworth, Royal Albert Hall and Madison Square Garden, so it's a little surprising that at no point did they achieve the top spot. They were never a band interested in pushing singles anyway, so who cares.

Green Day

For a band with so many classic singles that were promoted so heavily by their record company and MTV, this seems beyond bizarre and slightly unjust. It is a cruel world we live in.

Alicia Keys

Huge success, huge talent, no number one. There's still time,Alicia.

Bruce Springsteen

There's not as much time for veteran Bruce, but he's sold out more stadiums than he could probably count so this probably won't keep him awake at night.

Aerosmith

"Walk This Way" with Run DMC was a monumental hit which fused rock and hip hop for the first time in a big mainstream way. Despite the impact of the single globally,it didn't reach the top 3, in the UK nor the USA.

Amy Winehouse

Her time with us was short but her music will stand the test of time. It seemed at times that Winehouse was embarrassed to be so popular, so perhaps it was a good thing that she didn't reach the top of a chart that she didn't seem to have much interest in anyway.

The Stone Roses

A close number 2 with their comeback single "Love Spreads" after a five year absence, but the iconic Manchester band never topped the charts.

The Who

If The Who were to release a greatest hits album, it is likely to come in a 3-4 box set, yet the extremely popular London band never had a number one. "My Generation" came in at number 2.

The Cure

Formed in 1976 and still with a huge following to this day this has not helped this iconic West Sussex outfit reach the top spot.

Metallica

Metallica were spat on in the streets by their fans after they made their first music video "One" as they felt the band had "sold out". So it's probably best for the safety of the band members that a single hadn't gone to number one. Imagine the carnage.

Ramones

"Hey, Ho, Let's Go!" didn't go to number one, neither did the rest.

Joy Division

"Love Will Tear Us Apart" didn't even make the top ten! Very odd. The Manchester band made quite the impact in their short career, but chart positions clearly aren't everything.

Bob Dylan

This is hard to contemplate, as he's had hits since the 1960's and the term "icon" hardly does him justice, but never reaching the top spot leaves us scratching our heads.

Bob Marley

Classic songs, many singles, amazing career, yet no number one. The genius had other priorities anyway.

Björk

It's hard to imagine the wonderfully weird singer caring for a nanosecond about chart positions. So this shouldn't bother anyone.

Radiohead

Huge commercial success for years yet nothing even from the classic album "OK Computer" reached number one.

Pulp

Despite "Disco 2000" being one of the songs of a generation, it only reached number 7 in the UK charts. Pulp never reached the top spot despite their massive success.

Muse

Surely this can be rectified. They've had over twenty years of critical acclaim, but a number 1 is hopefully round the corner for a band oozing talent.

Johnny Cash

Another one to leave you puzzled. Scientists and musicologists combined couldn't figure out how this happened.

Guns N' Roses

The US rockers have finally reformed, though it is unclear if never having had a number one was the sole reason for doing this. There is still time.

AC/DC

There are no words.

Beastie Boys

When you sell 50 million copies worldwide, you would think you would have a number 1 at some point in your career. Not the Beastie Boys though.

James Brown

This is slightly more understandable given his singles weren't necessarily promoted to the same degree his albums were. Still, he deserves a number one surely? He's James Brown!

Dolly Parton

Poor Dolly, she never stops smiling though, selling 100 million records worldwide may be part of the reason.

8

<u>Nirvana</u>

Yes, this is hideous. Massive band, hugely influential, phenomenal writing, and if anything, it's about to get worse when you read on.

<u>Foo Fighters</u>

How on earth can this happen? Dave Grohl is the nicest man in rock but has clearly been shamed by mankind as we have never awarded him a number one single in any of his bands. Although it's extremely doubtful he would give it a second thought (A second thought to the number one thing, not being shamed by mankind).

<u>Janet Jackson</u>

She's the eleventh bestselling female artist in the USA and has an estimated 100 million record sales, yet despite releasing solo material since 1982, didn't reach the top spot. Interestingly, perhaps even Janet doesn't know this, as she released a greatest hits album called "Number Ones"! Obviously no one had the guts to tell her when she suggested that album title at the meeting.

Tragically, the Crazy Frog and Mr Blobby have both had number one hits. This doesn't help.

(NME, 2017)

34

Musical Anhedonia: The 2% Who Don't Like Music

To all of us who absolutely love music it may seem incomprehensible that there are those who don't like the art form. Millions are touched when they hear a certain song as it triggers memories from long ago. A piece of music can convey such emotion with or without lyrics. From a one hundred piece orchestra with a vast range of dynamics to one person singing a capella, music can be extremely powerful.

Naturally, some people will enjoy music more than others, but as far as people not liking music, it goes a lot deeper than that. Studies have shown that there is a very small percentage of people who fail to have any sort of emotional connection with music. Recent research has described this as a physical condition called Musical Anhedonia.

The research which included a study by a university in Barcelona, led to professors initially identifying that the individuals may have a disorder called amusia, which is an inability to recognise or reproduce pitch. They soon discovered it was more complex. To conduct the experiment, researchers went on to select thirty volunteers and put them into three groups; ten who said they felt great pleasure whilst listening to music, ten who said they felt a moderate sense of pleasure while listening to music, and a third group who felt that they had no real emotional connection to music.

All volunteers from the three groups had to listen to a variety of music, ranging from classical to contemporary. Thirteen pieces in total were selected by the researchers plus an additional three that each professor chose on their own.
There were also some physiological responses recorded from the participants, such as heartbeat, sweating and general human reactions.

What the university found was that people who had
previously marked that they didn't have any emotional
connection to music, saw no change in their general
human emotional responses, such as sweating, heartbeat
etc. However, the other groups who had outlined that
they felt pleasure listening to music did have a reaction in
their measurements of the autonomic nervous system.

There have been many other experiments of this nature
conducted with similar results. It must however be noted,
in a rather bizarre twist, that despite those conditioned
with Musical Anhedonia, this does not mean you cannot
grasp the principles of music. People who have Musical
Anhedonia can even have a thorough understanding and
appreciation of music. Many of them have studied music
at school and can play an instrument, they simply don't
have an emotional connection to it. They can see it as a
distraction or even be bored by it.

A lot of musicians will be praying for the day that a
condition named "Working-for-a-living-doing-a-real-job
Anhedonia" exists. They will be queuing up to be
diagnosed.

35

Famous Band's Guitarist Been Missing for Over 20 Years

As the nature of this book is overall light-hearted and fun, there was apprehension in including this chapter given the extent of its sadness. However, I was surprised when talking to people close to me, that there wasn't as much awareness of this story as I expected. With this in mind, any attention whatsoever drawn to this ongoing unsolved missing person case surely isn't a bad thing, as you just never know what it may lead to.

Welsh alternative rock group Manic Street Preachers have enjoyed a wealth of success since their formation in 1986. A younger generation will be familiar with the band as a three piece outfit, however there was once a fourth and very critical member of the band; guitarist and lyricist Richey Edwards.

Edwards was a highly intelligent and articulate young man whose lyrics meant so much to so many. The social and political commentary that the band's foundations were built on, is echoed in Richey's words. The group, who all met when growing up in Blackwood, had built up a considerable underground following in their early years. At that stage they very much adopted a punk style, citing The Clash and the Sex Pistols as their main role models. Come 1994 they had written, recorded and released three albums. The pressures of consistent touring and Richey's high expectations of the band were starting to take their toll, particularly on Richey himself.

This, combined with the excessive alcohol and drugs intake had those close to him extremely worried. This was made worse by rumours of self-harm and even an attempted suicide.

One incident that really had Richey's bandmates concerned for their childhood friend, took place in 1994 when the band were playing a gig in Norwich. Journalist and DJ Steve Lamacq was in attendance with the intent of interviewing Richey. The two got into a discussion after the gig, in which Richey and Lamacq began questioning whether the band had become too commercialised or not. Richey went on a rather articulate rant, stating the band were for real in every possible way. Whilst still mid-rant, Edwards took a razor blade from his pocket and wrote/carved the words "For Real" on his own arm, to the shock and worry of the journalist, as Richey's blood dripped all over the carpet.

At the start of 1995, Richey did seem in a better place as bassist Nicky Wire stated that the last set of rehearsals prior to their up and coming tour had been the best the band had sounded. He also said that the dynamic between the group musically and personally had never been better, with Richey in really good spirits.

On the 1st of February 1995, Richey and the band's frontman James Dean Bradfield were due to fly to America to begin a promotional tour of the new album, "The Holy Bible". The two were staying at the London Embassy Hotel and were due to check out that morning.

At round 9am, James knocked on Richey's door, but there was no answer. It transpires that he had left the hotel at 7am that morning and had taken his car. That was the last time Richey was ever seen.

What happened to Edwards over those next two weeks is something of a mystery. He left a note to a mystery girl in his hotel room with the words "I Love You". His parents let themselves into his flat later that day, to find his passport and wallet next to the bed.

To put certain elements of the story into perspective, dealing with a missing person was extremely different back in 1995. There was no specialist unit to deal with the case and given that social media wasn't around, this was not something the relevant authorities could have used to their benefit. CCTV footage was in its infancy and Richey did not own a mobile phone.

It transpired that during the period of the 1st of February to the 17th of February, Richey withdrew £200 from his bank account. He had travelled from London to Wales, then to Bristol. As a result of this, three different police forces were involved in the case, which unfortunately added to the confusion of his whereabouts.

On the 17th of February 1995, Richey's silver Vauxhall Astra was found on the Severn Bridge service station at the Welsh border. The driver's seat was laid straight back, seemingly to enable the person to sleep there. There were various food wrappers left in the car as well as a bag full of random pictures, none of which gave any hint of his whereabouts.

As the weeks turned into months, no word came from Richey and his family, close friends and bandmates were left to wonder. They decided to continue with the band, the first song they wrote after Richey's disappearance was "A Design for Life". The song catapulted them into new heights of fame, and remains their biggest hit today. Filled with the emotional strain of everything they had been through, they wrote the album "Everything Must Go". A masterpiece for their generation.

In 2009, Manic Street Preachers released an album including all of Richey's unreleased lyrics that he had given to the band weeks prior to him going missing.

He was officially declared "presumed dead" on the 23rd of November 2008, 13 years after he went missing. Despite now being missing for over 23 years, the band still keep an account for Richey, putting aside all song writing royalties owed to him.

The three members of the band along with all of those around him live in hope that he is still alive.

36

Greatest Scandal in the History of Music?

From Franz Liszt to the Sex Pistols, controversy and scandal has followed music since the art form began. From John Lennon stating that The Beatles were more popular than Jesus, to Michael Jackson's child abuse accusations, to Kanye West covering Bohemian Rhapsody (sorry Kanye).

Perhaps this next case is a strong contender for being the greatest scandal in the history of music. It is an extremely bizarre, sad, and arguably an unfortunate representation of the modern day music industry.

It involves a German pop duo consisting of Rob Pilatus and Fabrice Morvan, better known as Milli Vanilli.

The group, signed to Arista Records, released their debut album "Girl You Know It's True" on March 7ᵗʰ 1989. The ten track pop/dance/hip hop fused album was about to change the lives of Rob and Fab for the better, but then, unfortunately, for the worse.

Before starting a career in music, the two met in Munich, Germany, and had struck up a friendship, both working as models and dancers. They started performing as a dance duo, then turned their hands to music. After one show, they met German music producer Frank Farian, who previously had success with other pop acts, most notably Boney M. It was alleged that pre-Milli Vanilli, Farian had been recording artists but using different singers for the final mixes.

Farian, working in conjunction with US label Arista Records, offered Ron and Fab a record contract which would obligate them to record ten songs with them per calendar year. Three albums/years in total. He also gave them an advance, which is a sum of money an artist receives before any profit is made. It's the musical equivalent of a mortgage.

Now that you have the background, here's where it gets dubious and tricky. There's no disputing that Rob and Fab didn't write any of the songs on the album, and there's also no question that the tracks were presented to them initially as instrumentals before any vocals were recorded. However, the duo claim that Farian didn't even allow them the opportunity to sing on the record. Farian claims that he did but it sounded bad.

Professional singers John Davis and Brad Howell were asked by Frank Farian to sing on the album, but they had to tell absolutely no one about their involvement. Farian said to them that they would be the voice, but the faces of the project would be Rob and Fab. Given that this was around the peak of the MTV generation and there had never been so much importance placed on the image of the act, Rob and Fab were both extremely photogenic and there dance abilities ensured the videos were very aesthetically pleasing, but in Farian's opinion, the voices just weren't up to scratch, hence why he hired singers to record the album.

Rob and Fab initially refused for this to take place, so
Farian simply asked for their advance back. The duo were
reluctant, so decided to go along with the plan, in the
hope that they would sing at some point. They had signed
a contract with no lawyer, and also had no manager, so
overall they were very naive to the whole process.

The album started to gain a lot of success, and Milli
Vanilli were enjoying a string of hit singles off of the well-
received debut album. They were selling out arenas across
America, however given they never sang on the record,
they were having to mime every single performance, from
small promo events, to their own concerts. The strain was
beginning to affect Rob and Fab. On one hand they were
living the dream of selling out arenas all around the
world, but on the other, they were living a lie.

Events came to a head when the group were performing
a "live" event with MTV. The backing track skipped
during the chorus of "Girl You Know It's True" and Rob
Pilatus ran off stage and shouted at an MTV
representative that he was quitting the band. He was
eventually talked round to staying.

In February 1990, the group were awarded a Grammy for Best New Artist, but despite this major high, a major low was just around the corner. They had reached a phenomenal level of success, selling an astonishing 20 million records worldwide, yet they never contributed to one note of the music that they had been granted this most prestigious award for. The guilt was eating them alive.

Shortly after the Grammy Awards, a meeting was organised between the group and producer Frank Farian. They outlined their frustrations with the producer, stating that Farian had broken his promise pertaining to Rob and Fab being allowed to sing after a certain period of time. They wanted their vocals to be present on the next record. Farian, however, wasn't going to budge.

The producer came clean with the media that Milli Vanilli did not sing on their multi-million selling debut album. He outed them, and left them hung out to dry. Four days after Farian's admission, they were stripped of their Grammy Award. To this day they are the only act in Grammy history to have their award taken away.

Although they were part of the scam, Rob and Fab were in many ways the victims too. They were the real losers of the whole scenario. Farian formed a group called "The Real Milli Vanilli" which included all of the session singers that recorded on the album. Rob and Fab tried to continue on their own as "Rob and Fab", but after releasing a poorly received album, they hit the studio again. This time they decided to put their differences aside with Farian, and try to achieve the same fame that fell away from them so quickly.

Unfortunately, the personal life of Rob Pilatus at this stage was out of control. He had turned to drugs and crime, committing a series of assaults and robberies. At one stage he was even bailed out of jail by Farian. Tragically, on the eve of the comeback album's promotional tour, Pilatus was found dead in his hotel room in Germany. He died from a drug overdose which was said to be accidental.

Fab Morvan is now residing in Amsterdam, where he is still writing and producing music.

In relation to facts regarding Grammys, the only artist to refuse to accept their Grammy Award is Sinéad O'Connor when she won the Best Alternative Album prize for "I Do Not Want What I Haven't Got". She declined to accept, protestesting against the Grammys' "extreme commercialism". Here's a thing you won't believe; it was in 1990, the same year Milli Vanilli "won" theirs. Coincidence? Well this is your opportunity to start a massively bitter conspiracy theory online using numerous fake profiles.

37

Elvis was a Black Belt in Karate But Never Wrote One Song

Before we even discuss topics regarding the King of Rock and Roll, there's a few things about Elvis Aaron Presley that you probably didn't know.

Despite constantly being associated with Memphis, Elvis wasn't actually born there, he was born in Tupelo and moved to Memphis when he was 13. He was born a twin, but his brother Jessie Garon Presley unfortunately died at birth.

Another element of Elvis's life that perhaps isn't so well documented was his love of karate. He began his training in Germany on army duty in 1958 with a man named Juergen Seidel. After returning to the USA, his love for the martial art didn't fade and he met Kenpō Master Ed Parker at a masterclass in the Beverly Wilshire Hotel. Parker took Elvis under his wing and trained him for years afterwards.

Presley earned his first-degree black belt in 1960, and was later awarded a seventh degree black belt by Master Kang Rhee. Elvis later opened up his own centre, The Tennessee Karate Institute. He managed to factor some karate kicks into his live performances too. So there you have it, God help anyone who tried to steal Elvis's burgers from him. That is just a joke, respect to the King. The Burger King. No seriously, respect.

Presley had all the charisma in the world and had the looks and voice to match. However, perhaps the unsung heroes in his career are the ones who crafted many of Elvis's songs that will live forever in music history. Jerry Leiber and Mike Stoller played a huge part in Presley's success, and the success of countless others.

The way the music industry worked was far different in the 1950's. Record companies had teams of songwriters who would compose songs for the artists on the label. That still happens to this day in many cases but believe it or not it was much more prominent back then. The Beatles were one of the first well established acts to pen their own material.

The famous Presley hit Hound Dog (written by Leiber/Stoller) was initially written for an artist named Big Mama Thornton, and was released by her in 1952. (Windolf, 2009)

Elvis decided to cover it and before long Leiber and Stoller were writing songs specifically for the King. These hits included "Jailhouse Rock", "Love Me Tender", "Loving You", "Trouble" amongst others. Despite the fact many other writers composed material for Elvis, and he covered songs written by everyone from George Harrison to Don McLean, Leiber and Stoller continued to write for Elvis throughout his entire career.

One should never overlook the many other hits they have written for other acts, songs such as "Yakety Yak", and co-writes like "Stand By Me" written with Ben E. King. Leiber and Stoller's contributions to music have been recognised far and wide, perhaps most notably in 1987 where they were inducted into the Rock and Roll Hall of Fame.

It is, however, their association with Elvis that garnered them the most attention and critical acclaim.

Elvis went on to record over six hundred songs but didn't write any of them. He was granted one or two co-writes but even by his own admission he contributed next to nothing to the songs. Nothing can be taken away from his contributions in other forms though; he was one of the first superstars of music. He had the courage and tenacity to be different and stand out from the crowd despite the authorities questioning and pressuring him. He was a white man singing black man's music, which didn't go down well with many. Presley had an edge to his live performances that made him extremely controversial. His suggestive sexual movements onstage had him dubbed a terrible role model by parents across America. This is hard to quantify now as his performances are tame to say the least, in comparison to a lot of modern day artists.

He influenced so many acts, most notably The Beatles, Rolling Stones, Chuck Berry and Little Richard to name a few.

Not to mention, he could perform a mean karate kick.

Respect.

38

Kurt Cobain was a High School Janitor

Jimi Hendrix, Robert Johnson, Janis Joplin, Jim Morrison, Brian Jones, Amy Winehouse and Kurt Cobain. All of these musicians listed are members of the 27 club. It is named the 27 club because that is the unfortunate young age that the club members were taken away from us so tragically. Only 27 years in age, and leaving an immense legacy behind, but still young enough to leave us wondering what could have been.

Born Kurt Donald Cobain in 1967, the super talented frontman of Nirvana sold 75 million records worldwide. Nirvana were the forefront of grunge music, and remain to this day a hugely influential act for many bands.

But before the Seattle native was part of the biggest band in the world, he actually worked as a janitor.

Part of the company Lemon's Janitorial Service, Cobain's
duties included everything from cleaning toilets to
painting the ceilings of the classrooms he once attended
as a pupil. If you go back and watch the legendary
'Smells Like Teen Spirit' music video, you will notice a
dancing janitor. This was of course a joke reference to
Kurt's previous job. The job itself would prove critical to
their success, as it is where he met Nirvana bassist Krist
Novoselic.

After the two struck up a rapport, Cobain would go on to pay for Nirvana's first demo with the funds from his janitorial services. As Novoselic explained:

"Here was a man who would never clean his kitchen or take out the garbage, or do these kind of chores, but Kurt Cobain was not a lazy person. Basically he cleaned toilets – that's how he paid for that demo."

God knows what the moral of that story is.

39

Quickish Things You Won't Believe About Music

Lastly, here are some quickish-fire things you just won't believe about music. After reading this, be prepared to become the aggravating and unbearable hate figure who starts every one of your sentences with "Did you know…"

1. The world's most expensive guitar plectrums cost $5000.. These 2007 'Star Picks' were actually made from meteors that were over 4 billion years old. These Gibeon meteorites were discovered in 1836 in Namibia, Africa, where their sale and general export was banned by the local government.

2. When he was a child, John Mayer was taken to a physiatrist twice by his parents as they were concerned given he was so obsessed with guitar. Luckily everything was okay.

3. Before she was signed, KT Tunstall once performed to a man and a dog in a venue called the "Half Moon" in Putney. She recalls of the performance, "I don't remember it being at all depressing, it was actually brilliant!"
(Cowie, 2015)

4. None of The Beatles could read or write music. Plus, two out of the four were left handed; Paul and Ringo.

5. Rap stands for Rhythm and Poetry.

6. In 2006, a piano was found at the top of Ben Nevis, Britain's highest mountain.

7. Mozart was one of the first musicians to use a tambourine. Despite the tambourine originating in Egypt, the word tambourine stems from the French term 'Tamborin', which refers to a long narrow drum used in Provence.

8. Metallica are the only band to have played on all seven continents. They marked this by playing a concert in The Antarctic called "Freeze 'Em All".

9. A song that gets stuck in your head is called an earworm.

10. Eminem holds the world record for the most words in a song. He managed to cram a total of 1560 words into a relentless 6 minutes and 4 seconds of his 2013 single "Rap God". The Detroit native will be delighted that he has now been mentioned in this book twice.

11. One in one thousand people have perfect pitch. They are known as lucky bastards.

12. The word karaoke is actually Japanese. It stems from a phrase meaning "Empty Orchestra".

13. Paul McCartney wrote "When I'm sixty-four" when he was sixteen.

14. The largest human beatbox ensemble took place on the 26th of June 2017 and involved 6,430 participants. It was achieved by The Hong Kong Federation of Youth Groups.

15. Every single violin is made up of over seventy individual pieces of wood.

16. The London Symphony Orchestra was originally supposed to perform on the Titanic. They changed ships at the last minute.

17. The 15th of May 1997 was officially declared 'ZZ Top Day' in the band's home state of Texas.

18. The Red Hot Chili Pepper's singer Anthony Kiedis had two rather famous babysitters when he was a child; Sonny and Cher.

19. The whistle on 'Dock of the Bay' was added to the recording after Otis Redding died. There was supposed to be a vocal section sung by him where the whistle is, but Otis unfortunately died in a plane crash before recording. The whistle was added by Sam Taylor.

20. In 2015, Scottish singer songwriter Lewis Capaldi played in front of 8 people (including me) in a bar called the "Hug and Pint". Only 3 years later, 2.7 miles from the bar, Capaldi sold out two nights in legendary venue the "Glasgow Barrowlands", performing to a total of 4200 people. Lewis was also nominated for a Brit Award.

21. Brazilian vocalist Georgia Brown has the greatest female vocal range, extending eight octaves. This was verified using piano, violin and Hammond organ.

22. Boy bands are famous for their key changes. They tend to arrive typically after the second chorus. At live shows, Irish boy bands Boyzone and Westlife followed the trend of having pyrotechnics go off to coincide with these monumental key changes. As a result, small sparks would fly towards the backing band, causing very minor burns. These were known as "Key Change Injuries." This term was coined by Irish session bassist (and vegan) Tanya O'Callaghan who performed with both groups when she was a teenager. Thankfully no animals were hurt throughout the process.

23. The most lengthy vocal range of any human is a total of ten octaves. This was achieved by Tim Storms. He holds the record for the lowest vocal note. The notes are between G and G sharp.

24. Louis Armstrong is the world's oldest chart topper. He was 67 when he had a number 1 with "What a Wonderful World".

25. "Sweet Child O' Mine" by Guns N' Roses was written in five minutes. Slash once used the riff as a warm up routine.

26. Scottish band Wet Wet Wet share the longest reigning number 1 in UK chart history with Bryan Adams. Both achieving the number 1 spot for a staggering 15 weeks with separate releases.

27. Napalm Death recorded the shortest song ever released at 1.316 seconds. The single titled 'You Suffer', was described by the band as "utterly retarded" and "ridiculous, but it was hilarious". The band even released the song as a 7-inch single in 1989.

28. The shortest ever hit single is "Some Kind-A Earthquake" by Duane Eddy, released in 1959. The single totals 1 minute and 17 seconds.

29. New Jersey man Dave Lozzia attended a show in the Capital Theatre in his home town in 1977. He caught a drum stick from Simon Fox from Be Bop Deluxe. In the year 2000 he caught another one in a casino in Atlantic City. He decided to make a point of collecting signed drum sticks and now holds the world record for the biggest collection at a whopping 2956 as this book

is written. His 1000th stick was signed by Ringo Starr and his 2000th stick was signed by Stewart Copeland.

30. The oldest musical instrument known to man is an ancient bone flute found by Dr Ivan Turk in Slovenia in 1998. It is estimated to be around 43,000 to 82,000 years old.

31. In 2012, Beck released an album titled "Song Reader." The album featured sheet music and art only, with no audio accompaniment. Two years later a 'music' version was released featuring numerous guest artists including Jack White.

32. Despite being left handed, Jimi Hendrix played a right handed guitar.

33. Before joining KISS, drummer Peter Criss was in a band called Lips.

34. "My Heart Will Go On" by Celine Dion was recorded in one take.

35. Tupac Shakur is the biggest selling artist of all time in Africa.

36. Dave Grohl wasn't the first drummer in Nirvana. He was the fifth.

37. The only member of The Beach Boys who could swim was Dennis Wilson.

38. Barry Manilow didn't write the song called "I Write the Songs".

39. In "Bohemian Rhapsody", Freddie Mercury uses the same piano used by Paul McCartney in "Hey Jude".

40. In 2016, Mozart sold more CDs than Beyoncé.

41. The Aerosmith song "I Don't Want to Miss A Thing" was originally written for Celine Dion.

42. Bono is the only person to be nominated for an Oscar, Grammy, Golden Globe and Nobel Peace Prize.

43. Axl Rose is an anagram for oral sex, his real name is William Bailey.

44. Angelina Jolie's uncle Chip Taylor, wrote the song "Wild Thing".

45. Stevie Wonder wasn't born blind.

46. According to the Guinness World Records, "Yesterday" by The Beatles was covered seven million times. Official covers range from Boyz II Men, to Frank Sinatra.

47. The Parents Music Resource Centre (PMRC) issued a "Parental Advisory – Explicit Lyrics" on the Frank Zappa album "Jazz From Hell". The album featured a total of eight instrumentals, with zero lyrics.

48. Katy Perry started off as a Christian Rock musician.

49. After boy band Take That split up in 1996, a hotline providing counselling was available for thousands of distraught teenagers.

50. Queen never won a Grammy.

51. In 1972, Deep Purple were so loud that they knocked out three people with sound.

52. The Britney Spears classic, "Baby One More Time" was nearly a TLC song, but they rejected it.

53. Coldplay's Chris Martin has a First Class Honours Degree in Greek and Latin.

54. Harp Metal. The clue is in the title. It's a form of music that features the genre of metal played on the ancient instrument – the harp.

55. The drum kit isn't as old as you think! New Orleans' Dee Dee Chandler invented one of the first bass drum pedals between 1904-1905. The modern drum kit was further developed in the same city in the 1920's. That means that the drum kit itself isn't even one hundred years old.

56. Pete Townshend smashed over 90 guitars.

57. Madonna's full name is Madonna Louise Ciccone and she has written six books.

58. Bill Clinton played the saxophone (He's not bad at all).

59. Kraftwerk means "Power Plant" in German.

60. The Simpsons number one hit "Do the Bartman" was co-written and produced by Michael Jackson.

ACKNOWLEDGEMENTS

For the brilliant illustrations in this book, big thanks to Martin Kelly. He's also a super talented musician and a nice guy. Go give him a follow, and check out his music and art as they are both equally awesome. Thanks for all the hard work Martin.

Instagram @Martinkellymusic

She's a remote working copywriter with a travel and book obsession, and her name is Caitlin McAllister. She's a top singer and dead smart. She proof read this book, thanks a bunch Caitlin. Go give her a follow and check out her blog.

Instagram @caitmca

ENCORE

Once again, thank you very much for taking the time to read my book. A lot of time, effort and energy went into this, so I really hope you have enjoyed it. Unless you are a psycho, follow me online, as I would love to hear from you.

www.scottcowie.com

Instagram @Scowiemusic

Bibliography

Books

Alison E. Arnold and Jonathan C. Kramer (2016). *What in the World is Music?* New York: Routledge. 193-203.

Philip Ball (2010). *The Music Instinct - How music works and why we can't do without it.* London: The Bodley Head. 40-63.

Howard Goodall (2013). *The Story Of Music.* London: Chatto and Windus Vintage. 250-264.

Kepler, J. (1619). *Harmonices Mundi.* Berlin: Linz.

John Powell (2017). *Why We Love Music.* London: John Murray. 181-210.

Websites

Cooper, L. (2015). Retrieved from https://www.nme.com: https://www.nme.com/news/music/various-artists-1075-1221250

Cowie, S. (2015, May). Retrieved from www.scottcowie.com: http://www.scottcowie.com/podcasts/

NME. (2017). Retrieved from www.nme.com: https://www.nme.com/photos/23-massive-artists-who-somehow-never-scored-a-uk-number-one-1422890

Sherwin, A. (2014). Retrieved from www.independent.co.uk: https://www.independent.co.uk/arts-entertainment/music/news/bob-marley-no-woman-no-cry-royalties-dispute-opens-at-high-court-9364763.html

Vincent, A. (2016). *www.telegraph.co.uk.* Retrieved from https://www.telegraph.co.uk/music/news/Happy-Birthday-song-and-its-strange-past/

Windolf, J. (2009). Retrieved from nytimes.com: https://www.nytimes.com/2009/06

Printed in Great Britain
by Amazon

55136706R00104